IN BUSINESS
FOR YOURSELF

IN BUSINESS
FOR YOURSELF

A Guide to Starting
A Small Business and
Running It Your Way

JEROME GOLDSTEIN

CHARLES SCRIBNER'S SONS   NEW YORK

Library of Congress Cataloging in Publication Data

Goldstein, Jerome, 1931–
  In business for yourself.

  Bibliography: p.
  Includes index.
  1. Small business—United States.
  2. Vocational guidance—United States. I. Title.
  HD2346.U5G64 1982   658'.022   81-21256
  ISBN 0-684-17436-7   AACR2

Printed in the United States of America.

Acknowledgments

Special thanks to the staff of *In Business* magazine and to the following writers whose articles about new businesses and their creators are included in this book:

Peter Barnes: The Solar Center; Tom Bender: Jobs Humbug!; Fred Beste: "Are You an Entrepreneur?"; Don Cunnion: Shepherd's Restaurant, Great Valley Mills; Mary Kentra Ericsson: Love-Built Toys & Crafts, Inc.; Frank Farwell: Wind power; Judith Gaines: Rural enterprises owned by women; Nora Goldstein: Great Lakes Energy Systems, Straub Brewery, the Party Box; Bill Grabin: Renaissance Greeting Cards; Joel Grossman: Hydro Spa West, Rincon-Vitova Insectaries, Inc.; Carter Henderson: Shelter Institute, Curtis Circus; Bill Hogan: The Red Balloon; James Howard: Changing business goals and functions; Kris Hundley: Chester Inn; Anna Carr Kodama: Research for "What Makes an Entrepreneur?"; Joseph Kascmer: Just Desserts; Michael Ketcher: Starting up for under $500; Terry Lawhead: North Country Book Express; Richard Leviton: New England Soy Dairy; Paul Lipke: Old Wharf Dory Co.; Grier Lowry: Johnson Fabric Farm; J. Tevere MacFadyen: Baldwin Hill Bakery, Cummington Farm Ski Touring Center, Crockergraphics, Frameworks, Susan

v

Riecken's calendars; Kennedy P. Maize: Craftworks, Red Lion Farm; Stewart Perry: The New Small Business Movement; Nancy Roberts: Crate Prospects; Ernest H. Schell: Antioch Bookplate Co., South Street, Microcosmia, Inc.; Robert Sollen: Animal Town Game Co.; Laurel Shaw Sorenson: Brookstone mail order tools and gifts; Don Stone: "Plumbing Your Cash Flow"; Eugenie Wallas: Birch Hill Builders; Malcolm Wells: "Underground Architecture"; Nancy White: A Betterway day care center.

I also wish to thank Karl H. Vesper, Albert Shapero, Robert Brockhaus, Arnold C. Cooper, Ted Harwood, Benjamin E. Higgins, Justin G. Longenecker, and John E. Schoen, whose studies of entrepreneurship have been a great help to me.

Contents

Preface

In January 1978, my wife and I became part of a new entrepreneurial movement in America. I left my position as executive vice-president of the $60-million-a-year publishing company I had been with for twenty-five years, and we started our own publishing firm.

We launched *In Business* magazine in the spring of 1979 from two rented second-floor offices in a Victorian house in town. We had sensed the vitality and scope of new business activity that was not couched in the boardrooms of *Fortune* 500 companies or dependent for success on climbing the corporate ladder, and we intended to develop a forum for that phenomenon, which we referred to as "alternative human-scale entrepreneuring."

We started *In Business* with a simple premise: that there are both economic and personal rewards to be found in small-scale businesses based on the alternatives being sought by millions of Americans in health services, food production, energy sources, education, and many other areas. Because of my own long-term involvement in appropriate technology, our editorial thrust was originally toward businesses involved with waste recycling, biological agriculture, natural foods, and solar energy. But gradually our focus shifted from specific alternative businesses to the *spirit* of the people who were developing alternative businesses. Scale and personal attitude have become more important editorial criteria than specific products and services.

A corollary theme of *In Business*, one that we consider just as important as establishing the economic relevance of alternative products and services, is that a successful firm can be built using alternative approaches to business. A thriving specialty restaurant can come out of a kitchen, just as a manufacturing operation can evolve out of a garage. Our message continues to be that gradual, careful growth makes it possible to sidestep most of the early pressures usually caused by high interest loans, outside investors who want a quick profit, or excessive promotion expense to gain a quick market position. At the same time, we emphasize, a backyard approach does not necessarily mean a half-hearted effort or limited growth potential. But we find in our business, as others have found in theirs, that it pays to reach the first hundred thousand dollars in sales before you start managing and staffing as if you had passed the first million.

This book describes what we have discovered about America's new small business movement and the people behind it. Whether launching a home-based sideline business or a futuristic solar energy firm, these people have much in common, and it's not an MBA from Harvard, Northwestern, or Stanford, or an obsession with return on investment. What these people share is a deep commitment to using personal talents as the heart of an economically sound enterprise. In most of the businesses we will describe, as in our own publishing company, the ventures are logical extensions of an individual's past experiences and preferences. Usually they involve a strong commitment to self-expression and product quality and a desire to derive personal satisfaction from one's livelihood.

The challenge, of course, is to make the personal effort pay off in dollars and cents. The purpose of this book is to share what we have learned in the first two years of publishing *In Business*—both from our own experience and from those of our contributors—so that people considering or starting their own alternative businesses can avoid the common traps and hang on until talent and instinct do succeed in the market-place.

IN BUSINESS FOR YOURSELF

1

New Business Styles

An exciting movement is beginning in America today: Hundreds of thousands of men and women are starting new businesses outside the mainstream of the economy. To most economic analysts, though, these people don't exist; they are considered aberrations, business oddities with little impact on statistics, on job creation, or on the gross national product. Despite the rhetoric of the White House Conference on Small Business and such agencies as the Small Business Administration and the U.S. Chamber of Commerce, these new entrepreneurs go their own ways outside official channels. At a time when centralization of financial power is increasing, these Americans plow steadily ahead, independently, many barely making it, many flourishing.

THE NEW BUSINESSPEOPLE

The "baby boom" generation has much to do with this new business phenomenon. The demographic bulge caused by the

1

extraordinary number of births between 1946 and 1966 constitutes one-third of the population of the United States and Canada. Having made its mark on the educational system, this generation is now wreaking havoc in the job market. There are just not enough jobs to go around—especially, not enough of the type to satisfy the large numbers of highly educated twenty- to thirty-year-olds. In his book *The Big Generation* (McClelland & Stewart, Ltd., 1980), John Kettle documents what we personally have observed: Many of today's graduates must work below their achievement levels, a particularly frustrating situation for a generation whose work ethic emphasizes job satisfaction over pay. Given this work ethic and the shortage of satisfying jobs, it is readily understandable that increasing numbers of men and women are starting their own businesses.

But the baby boom generation is not the only segment of our society causing the surge in new business. My wife and I, in our early fifties, hardly classify even as late-blooming baby boomers, but we do fit into another category: the "now or never" group who decide to leave an executive position and start out fresh. Often people in this age bracket launch the enterprise in close cooperation with members of the younger generation—their own children, to be exact.

Still another age group has had a major impact on the increasing ranks of new businesses: retirees who create part-time and full-time enterprises as a way to cope with inflation and maintain their zest for life. Together, these different age groups are creating a new business movement in America, with styles that are unique.

The people who make up the small business movement are all concerned with profits and cash flow, but few are obsessed with maximizing the "bottom line." Although they usually don't have the time or the inclination to do a song and dance about how socially relevant their business is, they know how it fits into the world around them—especially their personal worlds. They are capable people and pleased to be self-

employed. And few fit anyone's stereotype of a businessperson.

Most of these women and men are glad to be on their own
despite the unsettled economics of these times. Typical are
Tom and Betsey Guido, who left Cleveland, Ohio, five years
ago to start a "dream" business in a rural location—a thirty-
one-room inn in Chester, Vermont (see their story on page
120). "There have been many times when we've thought of
leaving—usually late at night after an especially bad day,"
admits Tom Guido. "But by morning we're ready to start
again."

We've heard that same comment repeatedly and have said
it ourselves. But such statements don't diminish the incredible
optimism of most of today's new business launchers. Neither
recession, stagflation, high interest rates, nor work-filled
weekends will dissipate the confidence that economic success
awaits us.

This kind of optimism has traditionally been a key factor
in entrepreneurial activity. The difference today is that financial success is not the obsession that got the movement started
in the first place. Despite the optimism, it's still a big surprise
when profits start building up.

In a piece for *In Business* entitled "Jobs, Humbug!" Tom
Bender, who edited *Rain* magazine for many years, sums up
many excellent arguments for self-employment.

Do we need jobs? Should we want jobs? Are jobs a desirable
part of life, liberty, and our pursuit of happiness? Or are jobs
a dead-end trap in themselves?

Having a job means working for someone else. It means
getting locked into one specific pattern of providing for our
needs that may be particularly socially destructive, emotionally
unsatisfying, and wasteful. Jobs may be a good option in some
situations, but we usually ignore the alternatives, which are
often better.

Self-employment avoids the division of interest between

worker and management. You've no one to get mad at but yourself, and there's no profit in trying to pull one over on yourself. Self-reliance goes even further, in eliminating the split between the producer and consumer. You know what you're getting, and the price is right, because the price is whether you're willing to put in the necessary work to do it! Self-restraint takes us another important step towards surmounting divisive conflicts of interest. Demanding less and thereby avoiding unnecessary production and consumption lessens our demands upon our resources and each other, lessening the conflict between us and our grandchildren for limited resources and between our greed and the health of our surroundings.

Many businesses are home-based and involve entire families—reminiscent of long-gone cottage industry. In *The Third Wave* (William Morrow & Co., 1980), Alvin Toffler foresees a tremendous shift of work into homes, a trend that will have major impact on production and taxation systems, education, downtown real estate, and suburbia. In *Home, Inc.* (Doubleday & Co., 1975), Scott Burns predicts:

> America is not going to be transformed by greening, blueing, drugs, magic, pure love or a more equal distribution of orgasms. America is going to be transformed by nothing more nor less than the inevitable maturation and decline of the market economy. The instrument for this positive change will be the household, the family, revitalized as a powerful and relatively autonomous productive unit.

ENTREPRENEURIAL ECOLOGY

An important aspect of many new businesses is their adherence not to standard business practices but to an inner logic, which we call entrepreneurial ecology, based on the skills and desires of the people involved. The more we develop our own publishing business and contact others in various stages of developing and managing an enterprise, the more we come to appreciate the significance of the basic law of ecology: Everything is connected to everything else. In the years since we started our company, we have found time and again that the more compatible an effort is with our own style and with what we have done in the past, the better the results.

When we were in the initial stages of publishing our magazine, *In Business,* a longtime friend who has his own advertising agency in New York suggested we get some free advice from a friend of his, a full-fledged professional with years of publishing experience. After my ten-minute explanation of our concept for the magazine, he gave me three words of advice: "Don't do it!" Then he qualified his advice: "unless you have $2 million and can raise another $2 million." Having neither the first two nor the second, we could only thank him for his time, take a long walk, return to Pennsylvania, and start the magazine despite his professional opinion.

After several years of publishing *In Business,* we can't say for sure that the expert is wrong (although I'm personally convinced of it), but I do know that launching the kind of small business magazine we envisioned according to the tightly scripted, computer-modeled lines he had in mind would have violated our personal entrepreneurial ecology. We would not have known the proper way to raise that much money, to spend that amount effectively, or to manage the dynamic factors that come into play immediately, such as advertisers, subscription promotion mailings, production schedules, and staffing. So we started with less than ten percent of that amount and with a staff of four very busy people with varying experience. The staff has now grown to seven, and the on-the-job experience is substantial. It's utterly unrealistic for any magazine publisher—large or small—to be overly sanguine about the future just a few years after the magazine's birth, but we have grown enough and had sufficient positive reaction to prove the economic sense of the route we've taken. We have done what we know how to do and enjoy doing, and we have been successful. There is no doubt in our case that following the idea of entrepreneurial ecology has worked.

After interviewing many hundreds of successful small businesspersons, I have come to the conclusion that an instinctive sense of entrepreneurial ecology is an essential part of the new business styles that are making their mark—far more important than a calculated business plan. Albert Shapero, who holds the American Free Enterprise System chair at the Ohio State University, maintains that although companies that plan do better than those that don't, companies *never* follow their plans anyway.

> The world is a great big open system with millions of variables interacting in intricate ways. Some Japanese inventor is completing a dream in a garage that may destroy your industry tomorrow. He, your competitor, and God did not fit in your planning exercise. It is the ultimate of conceit to think that the world can be encompassed in the plan, which is a product of your desires and limited knowledge.

Entrepreneurial ecology is concerned with the personal relationship between the owner and the business, as well as with the broader relationship between the business and society and the physical environment. Managing a business on ecological principles may well add up to short-term frustrations. In contrast to some supposedly sure-fire managing-by-objective lectures we've heard, managing-by-ecology will force you to juggle numbers with deep-felt personal beliefs as you probe the priorities of interrelationships. But frustrations and mental gymnastics are a relatively small price to pay for winding up where you really wanted to be when you started out.

A major reason why American business is in trouble right now is that most *Fortune* 500 company executives disdain anything that might reduce short-term or medium-term profits. According to Michael M. Thomas, former senior vice-president of an investment banking firm and author of the best-selling book *Green Monday* (Simon & Schuster, 1980), "In thinking primarily about the next quarter's earnings, businessmen have very little grasp of both the longer-run consequences and longer-range possibilities." As a major step toward turning things around and getting young people educated for business careers, Thomas advocates closing every graduate school of business and every management consulting firm. "People go to the schools for a job, a meal ticket, and management consulting firms consist of people who came right out of those schools. So you have this unedifying spectacle of companies that have gotten into difficulty being prescribed to by young men and women six months out of business school."

Writing about the ailments of American industry, James Fallows of the *Atlantic* also cites the problems caused by unecological behavior on the part of professional managers. Many chief executive officers "want to demonstrate to their directors, their stockholders, and the financial community that this year's rate of growth is as projected, that they'll meet this year's targets this year. What gets lost is the strategy that will take the company over twenty-five or thirty-five years."

The people we know who are investing in themselves— who are living out their own small business dream—have clearly made a long-term commitment. They have resolved psychologically and financially to stay where they are, relying on a concentrated effort to find the desired market. And *time*—years of effort and a desire for a success measured in something more than short-term profits—is a major factor in entrepreneurial ecology.

The marketing function cannot be separated from the management function in a small business, so there is a single grade for performance. By contrast, the breakdown between management and marketing in corporations like General Electric, IBM, Mobil Oil, and General Foods has become so severe that their chief executive officers accuse their own marketers of being myopic, of lacking innovative and entrepreneurial thinking, and of running products right into the ground. One executive's opinion, reported in a study made by Marketing Professor Frederick E. Webster, Jr., of Dartmouth College's Amos Tuck School of Business Administration, is: "The way all MBAs, whether they're from Harvard or Stanford or whatever, approach a business problem tends to be relatively the same." Diversity, not uniformity, is another key aspect of ecological management.

In a small company, the connections between different functions don't have to be verbalized at daily or weekly meetings. The connections exist because decisions regarding, say, production and marketing, are made in the same office, often by the same person. Thus ecological principles are not superimposed on boxes in an organizational chart; they're intrinsic to the business itself.

The closer the connections between the parts of a business, the better it does during periods of economic change. In a talk presented at a 1980 seminar on America's new small business movement, Jim Howard of Country Business Services pointed out some changes in the goals and functions of business that are likely to arise during the coming two decades. Several of Howard's points are relevant to the concept of entrepreneurial ecology:

Quality The new market will be a quality rather than a quantity market; businesses will do better to focus on top quality rather than bottom price. Not only will this attract a real (if not usually recognized) growth market, it is also lots more fun.

Human Values As the economy becomes more decentralized, people are becoming disenchanted with the cynical, bottom-line, quantitative ethic of the big corporation. Successful businesses will be more personal than in the past.

Unifying Concept The development of a unifying concept for any small business is essential in an age when communication has gone wild. Develop an explicit message to deliver to a defined audience—otherwise it will never penetrate the public's growing resistance to proliferating messages.

Unified objectives flow naturally from the creative spirit of well-managed small companies. In the publishing field, for example, the specialized magazine often leads to the specialized book—editorial expertise can be communicated in book as well as magazine form. A market of readers for this specialized information has been identified, and the extra "product"—a book—can be successfully marketed. Whatever the term for it—entrepreneurial ecology, synergism, target marketing—it works for the small publisher. Today's largest book publishers, on the other hand, are straining for the outer limits—the much-sought-after blockbuster, the multimedia event that requires multimillion-dollar advances in the hope that it will be a best seller in hardback and paperback and then go on to the movie screen. Such an approach, by which everything has to fall into place quickly, is hardly balanced by anyone's standards.

Writing in the *New Yorker*, Thomas Whiteside reported on the troubles of the conglomerate-owned book publishing scene in a series of articles in October 1980. Whiteside quoted Roger Straus, whose company Farrar, Straus & Giroux is one of the few independents left among the major publishers, on the prevailing atmosphere:

> Concentration on the big book is at the cost of other books. ... I remember a conversation with a younger editor in which he defended the policies of the company he was with—one of the larger companies. He said, "It's ridiculous to say that we're not interested in books that aren't going to be really big sellers. We're always being told by the publisher to look for books of literary merit." But then he said, "Of course, we're told not to bring to any editorial conference any book that's likely to sell less than four or five thousand copies." Well, you can't have it both ways.

The men and women of all ages who are searching for and finding niches in the marketplace for the products and services they offer—the people who are using entrepreneurial ecology—knew before they started out that "you can't have it both ways." One holistic way is enough.

Carter Henderson has thought a great deal about the new business movement, which he refers to as New Age Enterprise. Henderson, codirector of the Princeton Center for Alternative Futures (now based in Gainesville, Florida), defines New Age businesses as follows.

These emerging (New Age) businesses are into everything from fish farming and life insurance to book publishing and solar energy; and their names run the gamut from the Colonial Broom Works (Maine) to the Sujimama Spice Co. (Florida). New Age and Old Age entrepreneurs share many similarities. Both, for example, are in the business of producing marketable goods and services, pleasing their customers, developing new things to sell, and taking in more than they pay out.

The differences between New Age and Old Age businesses, however, are more important than their similarities. Indeed, it is the very values and practices which New Age business does not share with its Old Age competition that makes it one of the more interesting alternatives currently being explored by the U.S. free enterprise system.

New Age entrepreneurs, to begin with, put a great deal of emphasis on what the Buddhists call "right livelihood." They will not, for instance, produce goods or services that result in the degradation of life or the ecosystem that supports it.

... New Age entrepreneurs are more apt to be personally involved with all aspects of the development, production, and marketing process than those laboring primarily for financial rewards in larger, more compartmentalized and rigidly hierarchical Old Age corporations.

... New Age enterprise is also proving to be something of a safety net for the free enterprise system, one that allows men and women to satisfy their own economic needs without relying on the mainstream economy that's increasingly being stressed as it attempts to find employment for more and more Americans incapable of employing themselves. New Age enterprise represents a growing source of U.S. economic strength and entrepreneurial vigor, one whose roots go deep into the finest traditions of American self-reliance and whose appearance on the business scene at this particular time in our history could hardly be more propitious.

Without doubt, the principles of entrepreneurial ecology are part and parcel of New Age enterprise. They go along naturally with the personalities that run the businesses.

We recently published an interview by Ernest Schell with Lee Morgan, president of the Antioch Bookplate Company in Yellow Springs, Ohio. For over fifty years, the company has dominated the bookplate and bookmark business. Employing seventy-two people, it has doubled its sales every three years since 1968, leaping from $352,000 twelve years ago to $4 million in 1980. Lee Morgan observes:

> I don't think that people should go into business to get rich. They do it because they have a product or a concept that they are interested in. If you happen to get rich, that's O.K. But that's not why you do it. If you're only in it for the money, and nothing else, it isn't going to work. You do it because it's fun and stimulating.
>
> I don't really give a damn about growth, but my colleagues do. You can't get good people and keep them in a stagnant environment. Good people like a little action, they like challenge, and they like opportunity. What we offer people is not the promise that we're going to grow, but that if they've got what it takes to grow, the opportunity is here. And you know, it's hard to keep them under control. You can't be sure where the growth is going to come from.

There's nothing static about entrepreneurial ecology. It's a constant give-and-take to find the right balance, and human energy and economic energy create a dynamic environment.

Blacksmith Pete Taggert's struggle to find the right business life style for himself also illustrates the shifting quality of entrepreneurial ecology. First and foremost, Taggert is a blacksmith, but he is also a businessman, a fact that he doesn't much enjoy. He's a loner who doesn't like dealing with the public, but to be in business he has to deal with people; so Taggert limits his business to wholesale. "That way I don't have to deal with nearly as many people. I'm a good blacksmith, and I have to be a good businessman, but I'm not a very good salesman, and this way I don't have to be." By dealing wholesale only, Taggert has found it much easier to let his products and reputation do the talking for him. "As a wholesaler, I'm only selling myself, and I can stand behind that. When you start dealing with the public at a retail level, it gets too complicated."

Taggert has parlayed his unique tool design and his reputation for dependability and quality into a business that in 1980 shipped out over twelve tons of tools. He notes that his dealers know what they can and can't expect from him. "We're just like Henry Ford: you can order all you want, in whatever color you want, as long as it's black."

To find the right business life style, you need a clear understanding of what choices you have and when to make them; trying to follow the rags-to-riches scenario has messed up many a business. Taggert knows about choices: "Making this business go is my biggest source of satisfaction. At first I just wanted to make it work, then I wanted to make it work and make some money. Now I want to make it work, make some money, and still have a little bit of time for vacation. You have to plan in advance to make it work like you want it to work." Now there's the mark of a true entrepreneurial ecologist!

2

What Makes
an Entrepreneur?

In March 1980, psychologists and business analysts met at Baylor University to share the results of their research into the nature of entrepreneurship. The organizers of the program, Karl Vesper, Don Sexton, and Cal Kent, had invited the editors of several national business publications to attend. For two days, we listened to knowledgeable academicians analyze the individualized, chaotic world of the entrepreneur. The experience was enthralling—a bit like watching a dissection of a small-businessperson. They probed to discover what makes the entrepreneur tick or not tick, why one flourishes in an environment that troubles another, and the training, or lack of it, that leads to vibrant health. Then they tried to figure out how they could reassemble the pieces they had found into a model entrepreneur whose attributes they could study, then teach to would-be entrepreneurs.

I've been to academic "probing" sessions before, and often the declarations quickly became tedious, especially when simple human efforts were expressed in complicated rhetoric. For the most part, the Baylor sessions had none of that; most of the professors recognized the immense difficulty of generalizing on the whys, hows, and whatevers of business start-ups and the minefields that can sabotage researchers, although a few did splash some jargon on their ties.

Small businesses confuse most researchers. Our bottom lines blend dollars and life styles, our business plans are buttressed with enthusiasm. Most business research is better suited to the study of single-minded profit objectives. However, one thing one quickly learns about entrepreneurial research is not to be turned off by its lack of concern for value judgments. It can give us a better understanding of what is happening, what kinds of personalities are involved, and how education can improve a business effort. As I sat in the well-furnished meeting rooms of the Baylor University Business School and listened to the professors discourse on the nature of entrepreneurship, I realized that the new small business movement does fit into this entrepreneurial arena, but at its outer edges.

In their discussions of new business ventures and the entrepreneurs who found them, many researchers look back to the earlier work of Joseph Schumpeter, a pioneer in the field of entrepreneurial research. His classic *Capitalism, Socialism, and Democracy* (Harper & Row, 1942) sets the stage for today's language of entrepreneurship and its research direction. Indeed, Schumpeter was one of the first to apply the term *entrepreneur* to an economic innovator and risk taker.

The meaning of the word is hotly debated by present students of entrepreneurial science: Some use the term to apply to any innovative businessperson who has decision-making responsibilities; and others use it in the strict sense of the innovative owner/manager who has set up a business or developed an ongoing business where none existed before.

Today, most students of entrepreneurial research would consider the owner/manager of a company an entrepreneur. But not all managers are entrepreneurs, nor are all owners or even inventors. The true entrepreneur has been identified by Benjamin E. Higgins, an authority on entrepreneurship, as

> the man who sees the opportunity for introducing the new commodity, technique, raw material, or machine and brings together the necessary capital, management, labor, and materials to do it. He may not be, and historically has not usually been, a scientific inventor. His skills are less scientific than organizational. His skills are also different from those of a salaried manager who takes over an enterprise after it has been launched. In any society, the rate of technological progress and so of economic development depends greatly on the number and the ability of entrepreneurs available to do it.*

Much earlier than Higgins, Joseph Schumpeter recognized the entrepreneur as the prime mover behind the "capitalist engine," as the creative force that drives the economy. Yet Schumpeter identified several factors that he believed would eventually cripple and lead to the demise of entrepreneurship. Intellectuals seemed to be developing a hostility toward capitalism, wealthy young people were losing faith in the system, government regulation was becoming a limiting factor, and inflation seemed unchecked. Even without these problems, Schumpeter felt that the entrepreneur would eventually die out as corporations grew so large as to institutionalize all innovative options, making new developments mere outgrowths of the company itself. There would be no need for entrepreneurs to start their own businesses: All innovations would be routinized by the research and development divisions of the major corporations.

The research presented by participants at the Baylor conference clearly shows that most of Schumpeter's dismal forecasts have not come to pass. True, inflation soars and the tax

---

*Except where otherwise cited, all quotations in this chapter are from *Proceedings, Baylor Conference on Research and Education in Entrepreneurship*, Baylor University, 1980.

structure may hinder the growth of new companies. True, the powerful corporations of the 1930s and 1940s—GE, RCA, Ford, and GM—wield plenty of economic clout. But do they really have a monopoly on innovation?

Mercer University sociologist Ted Harwood does not think so. Since Schumpeter's time, he says,

> [the] economy's cutting edge has moved to firms that were either hardly known to the public in the 1930s or didn't as yet exist, among them such firms as Xerox, Hewlett-Packard, Texas Instruments, Analog Devices, Digital Equipment, and Control Data, most founded during or after World War II by solo entrepreneurs or entrepreneurial teams, many working out of now legendary garage and basement industries.

Harwood's work in the sociology of entrepreneurship offers hope to anyone who fears that small business is on its way out. He claims that in spite of the harsh tax and regulatory climate created by today's economy, an entrepreneurial rebirth is in the making. Innovation is more necessary than ever before, and only the small firms can move quickly enough to make decisions on new products, production methods, and markets. According to Harwood and to Joseph Mancuso, director of the Center for Entrepreneurial Management in Worcester, Mass., the smaller companies are free of the red tape and hierarchies that delay decision making. Swanson, they point out, not the far larger General Foods or Campbell Soups, created the convenience food revolution; Texas Instruments, originally a tiny company in comparison with GE or RCA, cashed in on the semiconductor industry.

Not only can the smaller firms change gears more quickly, but they also have the advantage of a smaller investment in their established product lines; they risk less in devoting time and energy to the new product. Furthermore, when the business manager is also the business *owner*, the problem of demotion or punishment for a wrong decision is eliminated. Innovation can thrive alongside risk taking.

The renaissance described by Harwood and others does not end with the now-big "small" companies such as Texas Instruments and Control Data Corporation, or even with today's basement industries destined someday to make it on the New York Stock Exchange. Indeed, much of the strength of this rebirth seems to stem from the recent emergence of all sorts of alternative companies, many of which do not necessarily want to grow much larger or richer. Although some academics would argue that profit is always the primary motive, despite what the businesspeople say, others point to a variety of motivational forces including a disaffection with politics and a desire to develop oneself and nourish the earth, to explain the formation of these companies.

Research shows that negative feelings for conventional jobs and positive feelings for entrepreneurship are common among entrepreneurs involved in all kinds of business ventures, from high technology to crafts to retail sales. Robert Brockhaus, associate professor of management at St. Louis University, notes,

> An extreme degree of dissatisfaction with the previous job seems not only to push the entrepreneur from his previous place of employment but may also convince him that no other place of employment would be a satisfactory alternative.... The fact that fifty-nine percent of the entrepreneurs (studied) had the desire to start a business before they had a product or service idea, compared with fourteen percent who had the idea first, supports the concept of the entrepreneur being pushed from his previous place of employment, rather than being "pulled" into an extremely appealing business opportunity.

Indeed, the greater the dissatisfaction, the greater an entrepreneur's chances for success with his or her own company.

Reasons for this feeling of dissatisfaction are varied, but many studies suggest that education plays an important role. The average entrepreneur has 13.57 years of education, compared with 15.74 years for the average business manager.

Albert Shapero, a professor of free enterprise at Ohio State, also deals with the concept of being "pushed" from the day-to-day routine of a nine-to-five job into the less predictable world of entrepreneurship. Shapero points to the entrepreneur as the "displaced person," the man or woman who has been dislodged from a familiar niche in the workaday world. Writes Shapero:

When you go into business for yourself you trade off the familiar and the safe for the unknown and the risky. The new business is the only source of support for you and your family. You take on long-term financial obligations with money that belongs to relatives, friends, strangers, and institutions. You have to work fourteen hours a day, seven days a week, for the foreseeable future. And, after all that, the odds are that you'll fail.

Shapero says it is less often feelings than *conditions* that push people into the chancy business world. A person may become displaced from his or her niche when fired, or when the firm brings in an outsider to fill a slot he or she had expected to fill. He or she may be asked to transfer, the boss might sell the company, or a major business deal may fall through. In the most extreme cases, the displaced person is a political refugee, a Cuban or Vietnamese new to the country.

Even in times when social and cultural environments have been antagonistic to entrepreneurship, it has thrived in certain areas. Shapero cites the Middle Ages as an example of fixed social relationships. Everyone was identified with a particular group, and each group had a rigid charter prescribing behavior. In such a world, Shapero explains, the entrepreneurial actions necessary to deal with the unclassified was left by default to groups that did not fit into any of the established classes. The Jews did not fit so they took over many unclaimed or unsanctioned activities: moneylending, dealing in waste materials, innovating (the guilds forbade the use of new techniques, and the Jews were not permitted to join the guilds), advertising, cutting prices (forbidden by guilds but welcomed by customers, including the nobility), and giving credit. The outsiders could only survive by creating new roles or by performing roles considered outside or beneath the domain of established groups, or illegal but necessary (and therefore barely tolerated).

In a study of 109 people who had formed companies in Austin, Texas, Shapero found that sixty-five percent were moved to start their businesses as a result of these sorts of negative influences. Only twenty-eight percent were pulled into business by the attractiveness of a specific venture. The remaining seven percent were "between things," having just finished a job, school, or military service. Some of these people might have also experienced what Shapero calls "internal displacement": They realized that a change was needed in their lives. The individual might awaken on his or her fortieth birthday and say simply, "It's now or never."

Not everyone who has a boring job, or who feels displaced in some internal or external way, or who says to himself, "Now or never," actually sets off to start a business. Not everyone who recognizes an attractive entrepreneurial opportunity leaps at it. Most dream of doing so, few do. What, then, do entrepreneurs have that makes them do it? What separates them from the average Janes or Joes?

In an effort to find this "something else" and perhaps eventually to be able to teach the quality of entrepreneurship and somehow boost young businesses, researchers have studied the psychology of entrepreneurs. Some of the traits common to entrepreneurs are discussed below.

Achievement

The work of psychologist David McClelland published in his influential book *The Achieving Society* (Free Press, 1967), pointed to the need for achievement as a characteristic common among successful entrepreneurs. Although McClelland's working definition of entrepreneur is somewhat looser than that used by most researchers today—his included both creative managers and owners—his results are nevertheless interesting and important. McClelland defined individuals with a high need for achievement as those who wanted to be singly responsible for solving problems and for reaching goals they set for themselves. Such persons also have a strong need to know how well they are doing in their jobs. Entrepreneurs seemed, to McClelland, to have these qualities and hence should have high scores in tests for the need for achievement.

In his study of males through high school age, McClelland found that those with high need for achievement scores preferred high-level business occupations over and above the positions of specialist or professional. McClelland concluded that a high need for achievement would tend to direct young men into business careers.

Others continuing the work have suggested that if a high need for achievement leads men and women into business occupations, then achievement training courses might improve entrepreneurship and encourage the development of new businesses. Research along these lines over the past ten years has shown mixed results. One might conclude that, although owners trained to increase their achievement motivation *did* increase their personal income, the changes were not dramatic. Most of the studies concentrated on poor, uneducated people, and changes resulted in their working harder and generally following better business practices. As Professor Karl H. Vesper of the University of Washington (organizer of the Baylor conference) points out, further studies are needed to see whether such training would be effective with college students.

Risk Taking

McClelland determined that individuals with a high need for achievement also had fairly strong tendencies to select risky alternatives. Indeed, the notion of risk taking is built into many scholarly definitions of the very term *entrepreneur*.

The true entrepreneur will analyze all the risks associated with a proposed business venture and then decide whether he or she is willing and able to take them. On the other hand, some later studies suggest that risk-taking tendencies are not significantly higher among entrepreneurial types and, in fact, do not distinguish them from the general population. The wise, successful entrepreneurs, it seems, are not necessarily high-odds gamblers. In fact, some psychologists point out that motivated entrepreneurs are often unaware of many risks; they can't thrive on them because they are practically blind to them. As one academic puts it, "They knock hell out of all rational projections."

Locus of Control

According to Albert Shapero, one important personality characteristic of entrepreneurs is the degree to which they believe they can affect the world around them, their "locus of control." People with an external locus of control believe that life's rewards will come to them from outside forces such as fate, luck, or powerful people. Those with an internal locus believe that they can influence the course of their lives and, in effect, earn rewards. These people tend to be more self-reliant, to desire independence, and to want total control of a situation. Most people, says Shapero, fall somewhere between the two extremes. Shapero, in the study cited earlier, gave a locus of control test to 101 Texan and 34 Italian entrepreneurs using a questionnaire that rates individuals from very internal (0) to very external (20) in their locus of control.

The average score for our 135 subjects was 6.58, which is much lower than the average scores of other groups that have taken the test. Indeed, to my knowledge, only Peace Corps volunteers have come out more internal.

Locus control is also related to whether people think they might some day start a business. One of my associates, Candace Borland, studied 375 business school students at the University of Texas, using a locus-of-control questionnaire and a separate questionnaire that measured the motivation to achieve. Borland found that, overall, students who expected to start a company someday did not have a stronger motive to achieve than other students did. What set them apart was that they had a strong belief in internal control and a low belief in the ability of others to control their destinies.

It is perhaps not surprising that, when business school students were tested and compared with a group of entrepreneurs, the students turned out to be much more external, with an average score of 10.2. Obviously, business colleges are training managers, not entrepreneurs.

Independence
Closely related to the locus of control is the entrepreneur's strong desire for independence. Again, the work of Albert Shapero provided interesting results.

When I asked small-businesspeople in the United States, Italy, South Africa, and Brazil, "How much money would you take to be a manager in a large corporation?" the answers were always prompt and usually abrupt: "No way!" Some would counter with, "Five hundred percent of my current income, and I'd have to be in charge." When told they would be number three, we came back to the peremptory, "No way!" When statistics were tallied, fifty-eight percent had stated that they would never consider working for someone else; twenty-eight percent set up highly unrealistic conditions that no was likely to meet. Furthermore, when asked what they would do if their companies went under, seventy-two percent answered that they would surely begin a new one, as many had already done once.

Other Traits
Given that a need for achievement, a willingness to take risks, an internal locus of control, and independence have

been identified as the personality traits common to entrepreneurs, the questions remain whether these qualities automatically guarantee that an individual will enter into business and, furthermore, whether it will be a successful venture.

As has been previously noted, Shapero and others stress that certain conditions such as displacement or dissatisfaction are necessary before the entrepreneurial urge can occur. In addition, the work of Arnold C. Cooper of Purdue University indicates that individuals must have had some experience in the business or role models during the dream or "pre-start-up" stage of founding a business. Most founders of high technology firms have previously worked in the same industry; many other small-business owners have also had experience with the product or process. The combination of some education and three or more years of working experience seems most favorable for a successful new company.

Both Cooper and Shapero have reported that the credibility of starting a company seems to depend on one's acquaintance with others who have done the same. One study found that fifty to fifty-eight percent of company founders had fathers who had worked for themselves in such ways as company owners, farmers, or artisans. In some cases, the role model is another relative, a colleague, or even a stranger. Writes Shapero, "Time and again, we've heard people who have worked in small companies say, 'I looked at the boss and said to myself, if that dumb sonofabitch can start a company, I sure can.' People whose friends or former colleagues have started companies make similar remarks. Familiarity breeds confidence through contempt."

Education and experience also seem to be important to the success of a venture, although more degrees do not necessarily make for better business savvy. M.A.'s tended to outshine the B.A.'s and B.S.'s, but both groups outdid the Ph.D's. On the other hand, lack of any college education could be a very strong reason for job dissatisfaction and could provide the impetus to start a new business. Cooper reports, "The overall pattern of relationships is consistent with conventional wisdom. Despite some mixed findings, we can say that, in general, entrepreneurs did better who were better educated, who had relevant managerial and industrial experience, who had owned previous businesses, and who had systematically sought the advice of professional advisors as they started their firms."

Other important factors influencing the tendency of an individual to start a business and his or her subsequent success are, of course, the availability of capital and market opportunities. These factors are almost inseparable from geographic area and raise interesting but as yet unanswered questions about the creation of such healthy entrepreneurial atmospheres as Palo Alto and Boston's Route 128. Are these areas conducive to new businesses because of certain innate factors or simply because there are now a number of other successful businesses? Could other similarly fruitful areas be injected with entrepreneurial vigor?

In spite of today's economic problems, the lack of venture capital available, and the lack of bank support for new enterprises, there remains a sense of vitality in these regions and in institutions and organizations where a number of enterprises are being set up. Shapero writes:

> We know that some cities, some organizations are more innovative, resilient, and capable of responding to new challenges than are others. I'd like to think that the knowledge we are acquiring about entrepreneurship will eventually make it possible to turn a region or a town on by creating conditions that induce potential entrepreneurs to take action. Once there are enough credible examples around, the process should snowball without further pushes.

Two Baylor University faculty members, Justin G. Longenecker and John E. Schoen, describing "The Essence of Entrepreneurship" at the 1980 Baylor conference, included these views on big and small businesses:

In large corporations, a few individuals continue, from time to time, to exhibit an entrepreneurial flair. Many builders of conglomerates seemed to possess a boldness of action and originality of approach that recalled the old-fashioned entrepreneur of earlier years. However, the large organization contains forces that tend to stifle the entrepreneurial spirit. Most big business managers and even entire management teams are more bureaucratic than entrepreneurial.

In the field of small business, we find a division between entrepreneurs and shopkeepers. The shopkeepers use traditional methods with an established product or service and a predictability of results that minimizes uncertainty. The other category of businessmen who display more venturesome, freewheeling, and creative patterns of management are the ones who perform an entrepreneurial function.

Universities are only beginning to recognize entrepreneurial research as a viable, full-fledged area of study, and much more work needs to be done in the field. Whether entrepreneurship can actually be taught remains to be seen, but it can certainly be studied, and the results may lead to the creation of optimal conditions for the realization of today's dreams as tomorrow's thriving businesses.

ARE YOU AN ENTREPRENEUR?

Using some of the research cited above and his own experiences, Fred Beste—director of business development of Kentucky Highlands Investment Corporation and president of its Small Business Investment Corporation subsidiary, Mountain Ventures, Inc.—wrote the following piece for In Business *to help readers judge their entrepreneurial qualities.*

People who have built successful businesses are alike in many respects. Whether you analyze the founder of a major high technology industrial enterprise or a small town's leading retailer, your conclusion is likely to be the same: Both exhibit many similar characteristics that the experts believe lead to success.

What are these characteristics—and, more important, do you possess them? While it is generally conceded that some entrepreneurs are born, it is equally true that others are at least partially made. And, in any event, knowledge of what it has taken thousands of others to build successful enterprises should in all likelihood improve your own chances.

The discipline of entrepreneurial research is not a precise science. Indeed, you'll find mild to strong differences of opinion, and no one contends that his hypotheses and conclusions are absolute. We all know exceptions, people who break the mold at every corner. Lastly, although these characteristics do hold true for both large and small enterprises, the complexity of a business as well as the degree of success to which one aspires can adversely affect the fortunes of the most conforming entrepreneur. Nonetheless, I believe you'd do well to keep the following seven bedrock entrepreneurial characteristics in mind as you build your dream.

Knowledge of the Business

This characteristic may seem too self-evident to be worthy of inclusion here, but it is violated by thousands every year, all too often with failure as a direct result. Seasoned venture capitalists could regale you for hours with stories of plumbers who "always wanted to run a theme park" or retailers who "could show this town what running a bank was all about." Fortunately, such endeavors generally require substantial outside capital and so are never funded; perhaps more tragic are the cases of ventures that are not as capital intensive and can be—and often are—self-funded. Examples abound in retailing and service industries. The dangers here tend to fall into either a "grass is greener" or "hobby" category. The former are ventures entered into by those who naively focus on the superficial glories of ownership without considering the associated effort, sacrifice, and risk. The latter fall into the much subtler traps of confusing a knowledge of the nature of the business with a knowledge of business itself. As an example, an acquaintance with the likes and dislikes of every house plant known to man coupled with a personal household that looks like a thriving tropical jungle will not alone lead to success in the retail house plant business. Equally important are a knowledge of local market size, retail traffic studies, bookkeeping, merchandising techniques, and any number of other business-related factors.

Drive, Energy, and Commitment

There may be something to be said for being one's own boss, but there is much to be said for a regular forty-hour work week (complete with hospitalization, pension plan, and two-week vacation in July). Even relatively simple, smaller businesses can seldom be successfully built with that same forty-hour-per-week level of effort. Record keeping must often be done in the evenings and on weekends; for many businesses, Saturday hours are a competitive necessity; and worrying and planning never seem to get done between eight and five. Almost all businesses operate in a competitive environment, and free enterprise is an exercise of the survival of the fittest, so exceptional effort tends to rule the day in the long run. Especially during the struggling, formative period of a young venture, when (often unexpected) setbacks are frequent, there is no substitute for the small business owners who simply redouble their efforts whenever they hit a roadblock. Going into business without recognizing the personal and financial sacrifices that will almost assuredly be required is asking for trouble: Marital strife is a common result of entrepreneurial struggle.

Persistence

In a related vein, successful entrepreneurs don't give up easily when confronted with obstacles and disappointments.

Expecting a difficult time of it equips them to handle adversity; indeed, many entrepreneurs seem to thrive on challenge. This characteristic brings to mind the story of the man who, when asked why he was repeatedly banging his head against the wall, answered, "Because it feels so good when I stop." To an entrepreneur, the extreme difficulty of a task makes its ultimate achievement all the sweeter.

Self-Confidence

Entrepreneurs' self-confidence is primarily of the inner variety; they know their abilities and limitations and therefore the heights to which they can rise. Their self-confidence should not be confused with arrogance, nor is it based on fantasy. They are in touch with reality and base their enthusiasm on facts. They would never, as so many *would-be* entrepreneurs do, present their bankers with a profit-and-loss projection that predicted fifteen percent after-tax profit margins when the leading firms in their industries do well to realize eight. Simply by being in touch with reality as regards their business, the marketplace, and their own capabilities and limitations, they are seldom if ever subjected to major surprises, particularly of the negative kind.

Goal Setting

Another reason entrepreneurs are not subjected to surprise is that they know where they're going and how to get there. By taking the time to carefully prepare an annual business plan with supporting projected financial statements, they know how fast their business can reasonably be expected to grow given their resources and strategies and how much capital they'll need along the way. Their goals are challenging yet attainable given the considerable effort they are willing to put out. They tend, in the words of one successful entrepreneur, "to bite off a little more than they can chew and then chew it."

Risk Taking

Entrepreneurs are not afraid to take risks, but they insist on the calculated variety, and they avoid "double or nothing" opportunities like the plague. This characteristic, perhaps more than any other, requires self-restraint, since in the business world, disaster so often comes knocking dressed in the cloak of opportunity. An entrepreneur who is running a successful machine shop doing $20,000 per week of mostly $1,000–$25,000 contracts will turn down (albeit, with tears in his eyes!) a $120,000 contract, or even a $35,000 contract that has to be completed in four days, simply because he knows that either represents more than his organization is equipped to handle. Before rejecting them, however, he'll bargain like mad for a piece of either contract or an extension on the latter! Conversely, if the largest contract he has ever handled is $40,000, he may not hesitate to bid on one of $60,000 *if* his experience on the $40,000 contract was acceptable and *if* he is convinced that the characteristics of the $60,000 contract are such that his shop can handle it with a reasonable measure of extra effort. He knows that the wages of overreaching are paid in red numbers, and he'll not bet all he has worked so hard for on a get-rich-quick opportunity that may be beyond his capabilities.

Use of Feedback and Outside Resources

Entrepreneurs are good listeners and regard constructive criticism and feedback as educational. They realize that even nonconstructive criticism may contain some truth, and they are therefore less inclined than most of us to make the same mistake twice.

Knowing their own and their ventures' limitations, entrepreneurs seek help whenever they feel they are in—or may be about to get in—over their heads. They solicit advice from knowledgeable friends and advisors and are inclined to spend occasional evenings at the library studying up on matters relevant to their businesses. They are the antithesis of the know-it-all.

If, at this point, you are thinking that the model entrepreneur sounds like someone who just stepped from the pages of the Boy Scout handbook, you are not all wrong. On the other hand, it should be pointed out that the model entrepreneur has probably never existed and that another characteristic many professional observers feel is found in entrepreneurs is a sense of *situational* ethics.

The above is in no way intended to be a know-all and be-all of business success prognostication. Even the most cynical reader, however, will admit that there is a lot of common sense involved in what the experts say characterizes the successful entrepreneur. Self-assessment is the most potentially biased of any type of evaluation, but it is a worthwhile exercise to undertake *before* committing your family life and your future.

Lastly, after you evaluate yourself according to the standards set out above, I would ask you two things:

Do you *really* know what you are getting into?

Would you *really* turn down that $120,000 contract?

3

Successful
New Small Businesses

The new small business movement has nothing to do with national franchises in the fast food, car wash, dry cleaning, cosmetic, plastic dish, or precious metal field. Forget about somebody else's get-rich-quick scheme and put yourself on a get-rich-slowly route that blends your talents, interests, and finances with the right market niche.

Since we began publishing *In Business* magazine, we've been contacted often by people who plan someday to have a business of their own. When they ask us about starting out, we advise them to learn as much as they can from people who have already begun their own businesses. By carefully researching the doers, the about-to's can fast get a real sense of what running a small business is and what it is not.

By studying people who are currently managing their own businesses, you will gain a clearer understanding of where the opportunities are for you. I don't know of many successful small businesspersons who got where they are by copying someone else or a specific business idea. But I do know of hundreds who adapted their own creativity to the business approaches of others and then made a success of it.

I'm quick to warn people against jumping on a franchise bandwagon or, for that matter, a nonfranchise bandwagon. The people who contact us are generally far too independent to be happy following someone else's carefully packaged script.

The following capsule profiles demonstrate how some new small businesses have applied a broad range of approaches to areas as diverse as mail ordered handsaws and worker-controlled bakeries. These are people who have brought their personal interests—be they fabrics or publishing or unyeasted whole-grain bread, energy-saving devices or children's toys— to business. For many, the transition from personal interest to business took place so gradually that they were surprised to discover themselves actually in business. In the process, they created selling environments that violate the currently accepted rules of mass-market, TV-oriented merchandising.

These enterprises started out on a small scale, often right in someone's home. Whether or not to grow, and if so in what way and how much, has been a conscious choice, taking into account goals for human relationships and values as well as personal finances. All these businesses sprang from a desire for integrity—in the product for sale, in the way it gets sold, and in the personal effort involved in every step of the way.

All these women and men are in their own life style of business, which is not what the business schools categorize as a high-flier venture—the kind of jump-in, jump-out fling that you buy and then hype up before selling. But the business is more than a life style; it is also a kind of love affair. There are the heartaches as well as the high spots, but it's love that got them started in the first place and keeps them going and happy.

Michael Phillips, who helped to organize a network of California-based businesses known as the Briarpatch, wrote in his book *Honest Business* (Random House, 1981):

In order for your business to start, grow and flourish, you must love it. There are many reasons for loving business: the chance to meet a variety of people, to make a lot of money, to influence others, to travel, to change the world. To love business is to make a total commitment to its needs, which requires dedication of your time, attention and considerable passion. This love of business is vital. Our experience is that you *have* to love business to put up with the trials it brings you.

Here then are some special lovers and the results of their affection.

THE HOME

Birch Hill Builders of York, Maine, was founded in November 1977, by Eugenie Wallas. The company constructs timber frames both locally and out of state using heavy, native white pine timbers and traditional eighteenth-century joinery. Locally, Birch Hill services include closing in frames to weathertight shells and finishing home interiors.
According to Wallas:

Building timber frames and houses is a great business. My teaching and counseling skills are useful because it is a people- and information-oriented business. The commitment to invest a great deal of money as well as the number of shared decisions that must be made during the designing and building process almost always place a strain on the clients. Part of my job is to help them have realistic expectations about what a house can and cannot do and about the possibility of something going wrong and being delayed.
I encourage my clients to be as involved as they can, both in the planning and construction of their homes. Some prefer participating as little as they can; they just want you to do it all, and that's perfectly all right. I do point out that by being their own general contractors they can save ten to fifteen per-

cent in overall building costs. We even encourage them to be their own carpenters, working with us for pay, or taking over once the frame is complete. This participation can save a client $10,000 in overall building costs.

Being in the building business has opened up other experiences for me. I teach a course called How to Be Your Own General Contractor at a local university. In addition, I am beginning a second book on building and contracting as well as spending some time writing for magazines. My entire approach to running a general contracting business revolves around a central intention to provide structurally sound and attractive housing for people, and to help them participate in realizing that goal.

People have asked me, "Won't you lose business if you tell them how to do it themselves?" My experience is quite different. The more space I give people to learn and participate, the more they want to include me. I consider this an investment in future framing.

Maine is also the home of an enterprise that ties into the home construction business from a different angle. Pat and Patsy Hennin run the Shelter Institute out of Bath. Their school teaches people how to design and build their own homes for a fraction of what an architect and general contractor would charge.

"We've been profitable since day one even though we've never done any advertising," say Pat and Patsy.

"When Patsy and I started in the fall of 1973," Pat Hennin recalls, "we graduated 30 students all from around here. This year, we'll graduate 1,800 students from throughout the United States and close to a dozen foreign countries." The Shelter Institute's steady growth to twenty-eight employees and more than $750,000 sales in seven years has made it Bath's second largest company after the Iron Works, which turns out cargo vessels and warships.

The impetus for the Shelter Institute came from the Hennins' conviction, after building their own passive solar house for $5,000, working part time, that housing construction techniques had evolved over the years for the ease of the builder rather than for the good of the owner. They decided to teach house building as a rational process. They were certain that if people had the right information they could do a better job of designing and building their own houses to fit their site, climate, pocketbook, personality, and even fantasies.

The Shelter Institute's most popular educational product is its three-week Compressed Basic Building Course ($320 per person, $475 per couple). A more leisurely Basic Building Course designed for working people living in the Bath area runs for sixteen Monday evenings and includes two Saturday workshops and one Sunday house tour ($275 per person, $400 per couple). Students who have graduated from one of the institute's basic building courses can take an open-ended Design Seminar on Wednesday evenings, which walks them through everything they've learned about building houses on paper before they start investing any money in actual construction ($150 per person).

The institute also offers instruction in "The Fine Art of Cabinetry" ($85 per person, two evenings a week for two weeks, run in conjunction with the basic building course; and $220 for the more intensive stand-alone version, every day for two weeks). Students are taught the theory, techniques, and hands-on know-how needed to build fine furniture. Or, put another way, they learn that "cabinetry can be an artistic love affair with the sensuality of wood, or a practical skill to efficiently harness finite spaces in the home."

The soothing, relaxing, and healing properties of warm water that have long lured people to baths, saunas, and mineral springs are the basis of an industry in which the average hot tub and spa retail store is less than four years old and does more than $300,000 worth of business. Nationwide, spa and hot tub sales rose from 40,000 units in 1977 to 90,000 units in 1979.

Larry Davis, owner of Hydro Spa West on Santa Monica Boulevard in Los Angeles, started in the water business with an aquarium maintenance company when he was seventeen with less than $100 in capital. That was sixteen years ago, but this original company supplied the capital for the hot tub and spa venture, and now the follow-up of maintenance service for hot tubs and spas. "When the aquarium business became successful and was running itself, I felt that my time was no longer needed. I was looking for another business so I invested $15,000 in a hot tub retail partnership three years ago."

The original partnership grew to three retail stores, at which point the partnership dissolved, one store was closed, and each partner took one store to operate on his own. Davis estimates his present investment in the retail store at $50,000. Much of the investment went for the construction of eye-catching showroom displays. "To keep costs down I supplied much of my own labor to the construction," says Davis, who is also a partner in a construction company. He makes use of his contractor's license to do remodeling and install hot tubs. Adding these spa and tub installation revenues to the $540,000 in retail sales volume provides over $1 million in total sales volume. Hydro Spa's average retail sale is $3,000, and the installation brings in another $2,000.

Climate is no deterrent to spa and hot tub construction. While an open wood lattice summerhouse can extend the outdoor tubbing season, a solar greenhouse can provide a location for hot tubbing in the most inclement weather. Basements also present intriguing possibilities because of their high insulation value, especially if the hot tub or spa is embedded in the ground. "Also," says Davis, "the heat escaping from the basement hot tub will contribute toward heating the upper floor."

DO-IT-YOURSELF

A flourishing mail-order business offering hard-to-find tools had tentative beginnings in the country home of Pierre and

Mary de Beaumont. In the past fourteen years, Brookstone's inventory has grown to some $4.5 million worth of unique tools, gifts, and gourmet items stocked in a Peterborough, New Hampshire, warehouse. Corporate headquarters and management shifted there, too, after the company was sold to Quaker Oats in March 1980.

A Harvard University graduate who majored in mechanical engineering, de Beaumont has at one time or another done everything from yacht design to car sales, including work as an economist for the General Motors Corporation and as a production consultant on naval aircraft for the U.S. Navy. His childhood was spent in a French-speaking home. He lived in Germany and also spent some time on the Mexican border where he learned a bit of Spanish.

The experience in other countries meant he could read tool catalogs in a variety of languages, or at least "grope his way through a row of dictionaries." His experience in a variety of jobs meant he could connect disciplines—that he could see, for example, how useful a clockmaker's tool might be for a jeweler. De Beaumont studied hundreds of trade publications and communicated with trade representatives from foreign countries. He also experimented with unusual tools that seemed useful in a variety of ways.

"Doing it right" was something de Beaumont and wife learned as the business developed. As it does for other folks in the business, mail order gave the couple a chance to reach a broad audience while staying at home. De Beaumont is also convinced that, had they leased space in the nearest city, incurring the heavy costs of stock, rent, employees, and insurance, Brookstone would have collapsed.

Moreover, straight retailing does not have what de Beaumont sees as mail order's biggest advantage. "Financing is not a problem for this kind of company," he explains. As a "cash-up business," money flows in along with the orders, allowing the couple to finance the majority of growth internally without the burden of bank loans.

Each product is sold for roughly twice its bare cost. De

Beaumont does not waste his money insuring the parcels through the mail. Testing revealed that the cost of insurance was ten times the cost of replacing lost products.

Now, after the sale to Quaker Oats, de Beaumont and his wife will remain as consultants for two years. And then?

"The only reason for me to sell the company is to retire." And that is what he plans to do. "Why should I be someone else's flunky in my own company?"

The theory behind Frameworks—a custom and do-it-yourself framing store in Cambridge, Massachusetts—is simple. Considering the high cost of framing, owner Karen Swaim reasoned that people would be willing to pay for the opportunity to do their own. At Frameworks, as she envisioned it in 1972, people would frame their art, learn new skills, and save as much as fifty percent off the cost of custom framing. The concept sounded solid enough, but, as Swaim remembers, "We had to introduce the whole idea of do-it-yourself framing. If you're going to open a butcher shop everyone knows what a butcher shop is and what goes on there. But when we'd suggest Frameworks people would just stare."

Eventually Swaim's initial confidence was confirmed by the ensuing success of her enterprise, but when she first followed her husband to Boston from Dallas she hardly expected to open a frame shop, much less pioneer a business that has since grown rapidly throughout New England. "I was a math major in college." She admits, "I didn't know anything about picture framing or business!" As Swaim puts it, she was just looking for something to do. "I spent about a year decorating the apartment, but after a while I ran out of things to do, so I started looking around for something to keep me busy. I'd always dreamed of having my own shop; I guess I had an image of a place to putter about, put a sign on the door, and take two-hour lunch breaks." At this Swaim ruefully grins. She has devoted the better portion of seven years to Frameworks.

"I didn't start out wanting to do framing," she explains. "I just was searching for a good business idea." Through friends Karen heard of a successful do-it-yourself framing outfit in Dallas. The notion was appealing. There didn't seem to be any competition around Boston, so she flew off to Dallas to have a look at the shop. She remembers thinking that she might open the East Coast branch. That thought evaporated and she determined to do the thing herself when the Dallas store owner directed his answers to Swaim's husband and went on to say that he didn't think a woman was capable of handling the equipment or management of a framing facility.

His attitude lit a bright fire under Swaim. She returned to Boston and read everything she could about framing. She found a partner, and, although the two have since split in an unhappy parting, Karen recalls, "I wanted to start the store with someone, because I was coming out of the housewife syndrome and I still really expected a part-time job. I saw the thing as a casual endeavor."

Swaim is reluctant to report exact finances on any part of her business, but she will say that initial capitalization amounted to less than $20,000, supplied in thirds by the two partners and a local bank. Not surprisingly, it was more than a year before she took a salary from the store, but since that time the operation has supported itself, its owner, and employees. "There's only so long you can work for nothing," she says. "If the business will not support people adequately, then there's something wrong with the business, and it needs to be changed."

The Cambridge store is not a large room, but it is well lit and not too cluttered. The space is divided into two big work tables and eight small booths in which customers construct their frames. A prospective frame builder first shows the piece to be framed to attendants at the front desk who help to determine the type of frame and mat required. When sizes for these have been figured, the order goes to a workroom at the rear of the store where several employees cut all materials. This area is separated from customers only by a low counter. The visibility of the entire system at Frameworks contributes to its popularity with customers. They can watch their stock being cut down, the wood frame sections trimmed to a perfect forty-five degrees on a huge, razor-sharp trimmer, or the windows sliced out of sheets of mat board with special knives mounted on long runners.

When all parts are ready, frame, mat, glass, and backing, the customer takes them into a booth. Each booth is equipped with the tools of framing: a special vise designed to hold two sections of frame together at a right angle, seven little cups filled with different size wire nails, a bottle of white glue, flat wooden sticks for spreading and padding the frame in the vise, a hammer and nail set, needle-nose pliers, tissues for cleaning up, and, attached to the bench surface, neatly framed instructions for using the equipment.

Frameworks opened another store in 1978 in a suburban area near Boston. Swaim owns and oversees the two retail outlets. As she talks about the store, Swaim brings forth its moments of transition, rites of passage for business and owner. "When I got divorced," she says of her own moment of transition, "I thought it was my chance to go anywhere and do anything, an opportunity to change my life completely. And I decided to stay right where I was, doing just what I was doing. I'm really proud of the people and the store. I really love it."

All over America—all over the world, in fact—more businesses are run out of living rooms, kitchens, basements, and garages than any economist ever realized. For many people, a business at home makes the most sense since it's the lowest overhead operation you can run. Some businesses are especially suited to part-time start-ups.

Natalie Johnson of Olathe, Kansas, runs the Johnson Fabric Farm. Her shop consists of 2,500 square feet in her basement and sells mill-end pieces, remnants, and sample fabric cuts.

Johnson had always liked fabrics. Her enthusiasm led her to making braided rugs, then to teaching classes on braided rug making, and ultimately to starting a retail fabric business.

The Johnson Fabric Farm grew out of the scraps that Johnson bought for her rugs from coat-and-suit factory seasonal leftovers. The factories had tons left over from their season's production after she bought material for her rugs. On impulse one day she bought a tremendous quantity of scraps with little idea of how she would put them to use. It proved to be no problem. Friends were more than willing to take the remainder off her hands after she had selected material for her craft.

The Fabric Farm has two operations: a by-appointment-only retail store, and a wholesale business, supplying other retailers with fabric remnants. Inventory includes a large offering of wools, racks of men's wool suiting material, and bolts of polyester knits, cottons, upholstery, and drapery fabrics. There is a melange of weaves and textures, as well as designer cuts, left over from the latest styles. Small scraps are piled in barrels.

Getting started selling fabrics in your home does not mean immediate profits. "I tell these people honestly that if they need immediate income it might be best to forget it," Johnson says. "But if they have a little nest egg to invest, if they enjoy sewing, enjoy discussing sewing projects, are creative, and don't have to rely on it for a living, I say, 'Give it a whirl.'

"I caution them," she adds, "that for a couple of years they will probably be reinvesting the income in more inventory. But by the third and fourth year, they should be able to take some income out."

Johnson has one message she repeatedly voices to anyone starting out with a fabric shop. "Do it, but try to have fun doing it. Any type of business operated in a home can be confining. Get away from it sometimes. Don't let the business run you."

FOOD GROWING AND PROCESSING

Communities surrounded by small farms are more prosperous and desirable to live in than those dominated by large corporate-type farms. That's a major conclusion of California's Small Farm Viability Planning Project, which found that the family farm is "indispensable to a sound agriculture and prosperous rural society." That same conclusion was also reached by the first and (until recently) only U.S. Department of Agriculture sociological study, conducted back in the 1940s.

The technology task force of the California study team estimated that a $15,000 net income (not charging for family labor) is obtainable on fifty acres for most vegetable crops, with sixty acres needed for fruit and nuts.

Family-size farms can be economically viable and profitable even when not operating at optimum efficiency, the study pointed out, adding, "The evidence indicates that their production costs can approximate the production costs of larger farms." Some small farms, it maintains, can actually achieve lower unit production costs in vegetables, fruits, and nuts, mostly due to the use of family labor and lower overhead.

More and more people are beginning to recognize the opportunities in small farming. Confirmation comes from statistics compiled by the Census Bureau and the Department of Agriculture, which show that, for the first time since World War II, there has not been a decrease in the number of farms and farm families or an increase in the average age of farmers. In fact, the six New England states have had an increase as high as thirty percent in the number of farms since 1974. It's expected that nationwide figures will reveal a similar trend. Calvin Beale, a population analyst with the Department of Agriculture, whose figures five years ago first documented the shift of people moving from urban to rural areas, says, "There are signs of stability and growth in the figures now that were not present in the past."

On Maryland's rural Eastern Shore, chickens are big business and Frank Perdue is king. Perdue owns a vertically integrated chicken empire that has made marketing history in recent years. Network TV commercials herald his brand name.

Hundreds of growers raise millions of chickens under contract to Perdue, who supplies the feed and chicks and guarantees the market. A caravan of eighteen-wheelers rolls up and down U.S. 13 with the Perdue insignia on the side.

Bill Zietlow is a bit out of place in this empire. His four small refrigerated trucks roll into Annapolis, Baltimore, and Washington, D.C., with "Red Lion Farm" handpainted on the doors. And Zietlow's 12,000 chickens in the old brooder house behind his elderly farm house are a far cry from Perdue's enormous flocks. Even looks accentuate the contrast: Zietlow, thirty-nine, is a large, shaggy fellow who favors blue jeans and worse-for-wear Western shirts.

But Zietlow is assembling a business empire of his own that leaves him every bit as proud as the pugnacious Perdue. And Red Lion Farm is becoming as well known among the health food cognoscenti in the Washington and Baltimore area as Perdue is among Hackensack housewives. Zietlow's hens and roosters produce 150 cases of fertile eggs a week (a case generally being thirty dozen eggs), which Zietlow distributes to seventy retail outlets in the region. Zietlow's eggs are so good that he not only markets them under the Red Lion brand but sells them to other health food distributors, including the well-known Shiloh Farms, which sell them under their brands.

What's more, Zietlow grows and sells mung and alfalfa sprouts and distributes a number of other high-quality health food products, including cheeses and meats and nonhomogenized milk in glass bottles from a Pennsylvania dairy. Because his trucks are making the runs to many of the larger health food outlets, adding additional products to distribute along with the eggs only makes sense.

Finally, Zietlow owns all or part of four retail health food stores that are operating profitably in Maryland. All in all, the sheer size of the business that operates from Zietlow's comfortably shabby office in the old shed behind his farm house is quite impressive.

The New England Soy Dairy of Greenfield, Massachusetts, is one example of the emerging opportunities in the natural foods field.

Incorporated in February 1978, the Soy Dairy now distributes a variety of products throughout the Northeast and has achieved a phenomenal growth pattern. A traditional source of protein in the Oriental diet for more than 2,000 years, high-protein soybean curd (tofu) has been rapidly gaining popularity in the United States as an alternative to meat and dairy products.

Sold in eight-ounce cubes and having the texture of a firm custard, tofu can be easily substituted in or added to any recipe. Although its raw taste is rather bland, tofu can be grilled, fried, scrambled or whipped. The Soy Dairy distributes recipe booklets that show the food's versatility.

One of New England Soy Dairy's founders, Richard Leviton, has been serving as a kind of one-person tofu industry organizer, publishing a trade journal called *Soycraft,* sponsoring technical conferences that bring together pioneers and investors, and writing about the range of commercial efforts from soybean farming to soy delicatessens.

In 1980, the company arranged for new financing to allow for the steady expansion in sales. The initial capital of $50,000 in 1978 had been raised through private investments. As the dairy's founders discovered, banks were unwilling to come in on the ground level. "They told us they would consider us once we had a track record," recalls Steve Hassell, who serves as president and sales manager. "But we found it wasn't too difficult to get private investment when we showed a better return than the banks."

Good timing, efficient equipment, and a keen business sense have made New England Soy Dairy a growing and viable enterprise.

Roger and Ellen Sue Spivack also have their own food business, Deep Roots, which grew out of a natural foods store they started in Lewisburg, Pennsylvania. They tell their story:

As a way to add to our income, we began to grow fresh salad sprouts, caring for them before and after hours in the kitchen behind the shop. At first, most people laughed at us, we hope because they were unfamiliar with our product. However, the business side of sprouts looked good—fresh, local produce fifty-two weeks a year, minimum capital investment, practically no inventory, fast cash turnover, high profit margin, and no competition (at the time). We also liked being the producers of a wholesome, unadulterated product.

As things turned out, two new shopping malls carried traffic away from their downtown location, causing sales at their natural foods store to drop. They decided to close the shop, and the sprouting operation became their main business. In the first year, Deep Roots produced 200 pounds of sprouts per week. The second year, it was up to 500 pounds weekly, and by the third year, 1980, weekly production reached 1,000 pounds. By 1981, capacity reached 2,400 pounds per week.

Deep Roots' sprouts are sold to just about every restaurant that has a salad bar within forty miles of Lewisburg. Via supermarket distribution, the sprouts are available throughout central and eastern Pennsylvania as well as in the New York metropolitan area. Roger Spivack says,

> At the end of almost four years, Deep Roots Trading Company has finally become a profitable business. In 1979, our total annual sales were $37,671, and in 1980 our sales should be about four times that amount. We have overcome our fears and operate with a posture of success. We now take a more aggressive approach toward purchasing and marketing. Our employees are secure in the knowledge that this is indeed a growing company.

Craig Gillihan, Sr., and family operate Great Valley Mills, a flour-milling company in Quakertown, Pennsylvania. They sell a wide range of old-fashioned whole grain flour by mail to customers around the country. Grain products include such items as yellow corn meal and Scotch coarse-ground oatmeal. Nothing on the list contains artificial additives.

The customer list for Great Valley Mills is made up mostly of what Gillihan refers to as "hobbyists"—people who enjoy making bread and pastries from the many types of whole grain flours he offers. "They cook for fun and relaxation, not as a way to save money." To get the best possible returns from his mailing list and keep unit costs down, Gillihan has added a line of specialty foods—smoked meats, preserves, relishes, cheese, honey. He also features gift packages.

Gillihan's mail-order business is flourishing, but he still has time to go fishing because both his regular catalog and gift package business are seasonal. The gift package demand comes between Thanksgiving and Christmas, whereas flour customers do most of their baking when the weather turns cold.

Paul and Betty Keene started Walnut Acres in their farm kitchen in the central Pennsylvania community of Penns Creek thirty years ago—making apple butter from unsprayed apples. Currently, there are seventy full-time employees, and the natural foods offered range from whole grains to soups.

We had no business plans in those early days. There also was no appreciable market for more costly foods in our immediate area, which was quite depressed economically, so we had to find a way to reach out beyond our small limits. Someone wrote a note about us in a New York newspaper. As a result, people interested in obtaining natural, unpoisoned, unchemicalized foods direct from the producing farm began to write us, and even to drive the 200 miles from New York. Gradually, more and more people wanted such foods more and more of the time. We felt that for both their sakes and ours, we had to respond.

The years have shown the wisdom of these early seekers. Now we all know that we are being overchemicalized and overrefined. Food consciousness now stands countrywide where many of our beliefs stood long years ago. We know that the market for our particular type of food product has grown tremendously in the past ten years, and we believe our business will move ahead gratifyingly, growing sounder but not tremendously larger. It is good to have eggs in thousands of small baskets!

The purpose of the particular corporate farm we have adopted is primarily to insure the carrying on of the organization into a far future, long after the founders themselves are gone. In hopes of succeeding in this, we first created two classes of stock. Together these represent all the company holdings—buildings, machinery, equipment, inventory, formulae, recipes, mailing list, good will, and so on.

The 120 founders shares, worth one dollar each, are owned by Paul and Betty Keene. They elect four members to the seven-person board of directors. The board will go out of existence at the end of the year 1999. At that time complete control goes to the holders of the shares of common stock, who now elect three members to the board of directors. By that time, it is felt, the organization members then active will be far enough along in understanding and ability to carry along on their own, still under common ownership and management.

At present over 1,500 shares of common stock have been taken from the stock treasury for distribution to members. Of these, the five-member Keene family holds 500 shares. They cannot get more, as the highest number any member may hold is 100 shares. Each full-time worker, after meeting certain age and service requirements, receives five shares of common stock per year for twenty years. These shares are given without charge, but the value of the shares at the time of annual distribution is a debit against the account of each receiving member. Finally, upon retirement (or earlier separation of the member) the shares must be sold back to the corporation at the rate of twenty percent each year for five years. First the total debit to the corporation by the members for the given shares must be satisfied by the stock redemption of twenty percent yearly, at current book value. Thereafter remaining shares are bought back by the corporation at the current book value.

The present minority of the Keene family members in common-stock ownership, of course, diminishes in size each year. There are presently several other members who hold 100 shares. A number of persons have retired, and their stocks have been repurchased, according to formula.

Flaws in the structure may show up later, but after seventeen years of corporate ownership of the business we feel well pleased with its operation. It seems really to work!

Looking both back and forward, we feel the field in which we are engaged is sound. Its roots are in tomorrow. What better assurance could there be than that? To live always in the future is over half of the battle.

RESTAURANTS, BAKERIES, AND RESORTS

Cross-country skiing, unlike its Alpine cousin, is well positioned to increase its share of the winter sports market despite uncertain economic conditions, rising fuel costs, and gasoline shortages.

"We're the first area that people hit on their way north," explains David Alvord, who, along with Drew and Dale Dawson, runs the Cummington Farm Ski Touring Center, "and because of our elevation we almost always have snow. People who used to ski in Vermont, New Hampshire, or Maine are going to begin stopping here. We think we're sitting on a gold mine."

The gold mine is a former dairy farm in the Berkshire hills of western Massachusetts, less than two hours from Hartford and less than an hour outside of Springfield. Most cross-country facilities have tended to consist of a small warming hut by the side of a forest, but Cummington Farm is undeniably big.

The farm has accommodations for ninety, mostly in wood-heated cabins alongside the trails. The restaurant is housed in a cavernous converted barn and can seat 200 diners. Twenty-seven miles of trails are kept groomed for skiing.

Cummington's profitable first year in 1975 turned out to be an accurate indication of what was to come. "The second season showed tremendous growth," Alvord says. "Our skier days more than doubled, and that year we didn't even open until January 7."

The three insist that the key to success in a tourist-centered business is attention to little details. The accelerated pace stretched their resources and their patience, but it also helped to clarify their goals in a surprisingly short time. "That third year we started to see two things," says Alvord. "First of all, we saw that the return on our dollar was becoming really substantial, with big annual sales. At the same time, we weren't getting the return we'd hoped for on our summer camping activities."

The weak spot on any seasonal resort's balance sheet is what to do with the rest of the year. In hopes of bringing in campers, Cummington Farm secured a $150,000 Small Business Administration loan to improve facilities, putting in campsites and a swimming pool. But they found themselves torn between skiing and camping; they could not devote equal energy to both. "Over the past five years we've built up skiing to the point where we're an established touring center and recognized as such," Drew explains. "That has become a business in itself. It can almost be separated from the rest of the year, and any other functions we might get involved in." Wanting to remain committed to skiing but faced with both a mortgage and their SBA loan to repay, the partners are currently considering leasing out the camping wing of the farm to someone who would give it the same attention that they devote to winter activities.

Dale notes that although the restaurant is only marginally profitable because of the cost of high-quality materials and the fluctuating volume of diners, its atmosphere and presence is an attraction for the resort as a whole. "We've tossed it back and forth a lot," she says, "whether we ought to have a cafe where the skier could get a sandwich wrapped in cellophane and not have to wait for table service; but it would be hard for me to run a restaurant like that." Her brother notes the friendly attitude of Cummington's personnel, suggesting that it can't be taken for granted. "I think the fact that the staff cares is part of the atmosphere here. When a skier asks someone in the restaurant about a trail, they'll get an answer, because the person has probably skiied it. People notice that."

Alvord amplifies this. "A smile goes a long way. If one of our people has had a bad day, they go home and beat their head on the wall, but they don't take it out on the customer. We push it and push it with our staff. If a skier comes in and wants their binding adjusted, we do it for free. Little things." He goes on to outline two other critical focal areas. "We feel that good instruction is terribly necessary. If someone comes up here who's unfamiliar with the sport and puts on rental skis, goes out, and can't get up or down the hills, he's going to throw those skis back at us. And he's never coming again. So we really encourage skiers to take lessons. We hire a fine teaching staff, and pay them well." Finally, Alvord urges quality. "Professionalism is so important. You just can't seem like a rinky-dink operation. You have to use good equipment and keep the place in top shape. It may cost a few extra dollars, but it's well worth it." The reason these subtle things are so central is simple: the return skier. "It's one thing to get them here once, but the return traffic is where it's at."

To make it all possible the three owners reinvest most of their profits in the operation. In their best season to date nearly forty percent of their $175,000 gross went right back into the business. And because the business has grown with the sport, the three have helped the sport itself as well. Each of them is active in professional organizations, and they've capitalized on their own hard-earned lessons by forming a consulting group to advise prospective operator/owners of cross-country skiing resorts. "Our feeling is that the more ski areas there are, the better it is for us and the sport," Alvord says.

In 1975, Nan Rick opened her restaurant, Shepherd's, on a gravel road in Van Hornesville, New York. The restaurant fits in well with her long-range plan to achieve a self-contained sheep business on her farm. She was already converting the wool into a number of salable products, such as tablecloths, sweaters, serapes, and novelty items, including plant dusters made from raw wool. All these items, plus her own pottery, are featured at her on-farm gift shop in the same building as the restaurant.

It was natural for Rick to think of a restaurant as a way of selling her lamb rather than marketing it as ready-to-cook roasts or chops. She's a graduate of Cornell University's School of Hotel Administration and has had practical experience in restaurant operation.

As you'd expect, Nan's menu features lamb, but not just conventional lamb chops or rack of lamb. She offers unusual lamb dishes from countries all over the world where lamb is eaten more widely than in the United States. In fact, practically all of the menu (including wine) is international in character. Besides three lamb dishes, the menu usually offers three seafood choices as well.

To simplify menu pricing, Nan uses the "prix fixe" principle—all dinners, from appetizer through dessert, are the same price—thirteen dollars. "It balances out," she says. "Some dishes may be a little high at the fixed price, but others are a bargain. The thirteen-dollar price is computed as follows: thirty-five percent goes for food costs, thirty-five percent for labor costs, and thirty percent for overhead and profit."

On Saturdays and Sundays, the restaurant has about a hundred dinner guests. Weekday average for dinner and lunch is about forty diners at each meal. The average dinner check comes to sixteen dollars per person, and bar business is not a significant factor of that amount. The restaurant is closed Mondays and Tuesdays.

Rick doesn't waste anything if she can help it. Bones cut out of meat before cooking or left over from roasts go into soup. "Excessive waste can quickly eat into the profit margin," she points out, adding, "Net profits are low in a restaurant. That means close attention to details. Everything must be well organized and tightly run. These factors are just as important as the specialty approach that sets our place apart from the rest."

Operating a restaurant is a twenty-four-hour-a-day job, Rick has found. "You must be wedded to the job." That's one of the reasons why her restaurant operates only from April 1 to November 1. "The rest of the year, I get to live a fairly normal life."

The smell is a mixture of wood smoke and baking bread produced by loaves of Baldwin Hill Natural Sourdough Whole Wheat Bread. The names on the mailbox belong to Hy Lerner and Paul Petrofsky, who began the bakery and live in the house. The name on the sign belongs to the bread and to the handsome wood and stone building where it is made and from which the perfectly delicious aroma escapes.

An old farm on a back road in the central Massachusetts hills may seem an unlikely home for a commercial bakery with direct distribution to five states and a national mail-order trade.

From their Phillipston, Massachusetts, farmsite, Baldwin Hill produces an average of 8,000 loaves weekly. Their van recently began making regular trips to New York, supplementing scheduled runs to Boston and Vermont. They now have two trucks and also deliver to New Hampshire and Connecticut. Baldwin Hill services about forty-five stores in Boston, thirty in western Massachusetts, and sixty in New York and Connecticut.

The labels on the bread provide this information: "We bake in the traditional way. Using only organically grown whole wheat, sea salt, and untreated deep well water. The dough is kneaded slowly and leavened by natural fermentation. When the loaves are fully risen, they are baked directly on a brick hearth." Hy Lerner adds:

> What we really want to do is bring this bread to the people of this country. I don't know of a simpler way to say it. That's why we started this whole thing; we found a bread that was good and nutritious, and we wanted to make it available to as many people as possible.
>
> Now of course we think of ourselves as big entrepreneurs. We buy things and hire people, and it's what you might call a business. But I can't tell you how many thousands of hours went into this before we made any money. Remember, this goes back to 1972, and it was 1978 before we made what I suppose could be called a moderate wage.

There seems no immediate control on the business growth other than its owners' determination to remain at a manageable size. "Expansion is not inconceivable," Lerner says, "but building this thing has been like climbing hand over hand. Right now we'd just like to get up to full production before we do anything more." The two men have no doubt that they could sell all the bread they might be able to bake, and they are equally sure that well-run bakeries of a similar persuasion could succeed elsewhere.

Some 3,000 miles away in San Francisco, cheesecake—a far cry from whole wheat bread—was the foundation for another bakery, Just Desserts. Begun in 1975 with a favorite recipe, personal savings, and a $6,000 bank loan, Just Desserts is now a flourishing $2 million-plus annual sales enterprise that offers an array of home-style, intriguing desserts to retail and wholesale customers.

The owners, Barbara Radcliff, Eliot Hoffman, and Gail

Horvath, were able to keep their original debt under $10,000 in the beginning, as the three of them baked and hammered together to get started in their kitchen on Church Street. When they opened their store in the Embarcadero Center, it took $180,000 in construction costs. Today Hoffman is in charge of finances; Radcliff, retail stores and promotion; Horvath, special projects such as setting up the third store and designing training manuals for retail clerks; and Jane Fay-Sills, a baker become partner, kitchen production, with the title of executive chef.

Retail locations include stores in the Embarcadero Center and another on Pacific Avenue, in addition to the original one. They distribute to 100 San Francisco wholesale customers, mostly restaurants and cafes. All of the 300 clients outside the forty-nine-square-mile city are served through an independent distributor. Just Desserts appear on restaurant tables as far as fifty miles away.

The style of preparation of its twenty kinds of baked goods sets Just Desserts apart from fellow bakers. All recipes are made from scratch, an exception in a profession that commonly uses canned fruit filling and one-hundred-pound bags of mixes. The production room is like an oversized home kitchen. One bakery worker feeds apples into a coring machine, another patiently cracks egg after egg until he's filled several five-gallon tubs with yolks, then measures in vanilla extract before dumping the sweetly pungent contents into a giant mixing bowl full of flour under huge mechanical beaters. The staff of forty, most in jeans and t-shirts, works in a room the size of a large hotel kitchen and turns out 75,000 cakes and pies daily.

Even so, say the partners, "Most straight bakeries don't consider us a bakery. Bakery magazines talk about plastic shortenings and longer shelf life. The whole consciousness that came about in the health food industry has really helped us."

GIFTS AND TOYS

Renaissance Greeting Cards of Turners Falls, Massachusetts, started out in 1977 "as small as could be," reminisces Bill
Grabin, president.

We created six black-and-white Christmas cards for sale to our
friends (via mail order) and to stores throughout Massachusetts. Our sales force at the time consisted of one person, Melvin. Yet he was raring to go and eagerly set his sights on his
hometown, Boston, and its many card shops. We also enlisted
some part-time sales help, a few people willing to travel for a
week along some assigned route and land some accounts. The
sales went well, by our standards. By year's end, we had
grossed $18,000. The season had lasted three months: Septem-
ber, October, and November. The total sales included both
wholesale to stores and retail through mail order and craft
shows (both of which we still do).
   The results of these initial efforts (a lot of fan mail) encouraged us to move forward. By March of 1978, we had completed twelve full-color Christmas cards, bringing the total in
our Christmas line to eighteen. Yet our sales force still basically consisted of one. And how much could one do?

To make the shift from regional to nationwide marketing,
Renaissance decided after much scrutiny to use national sales
representatives, beginning with New England and then gradually making contact with firms in other areas.
   Grabin continues:

The commissions we give are fairly standard for our industry:
twenty percent on counter cards; fifteen percent on boxed
cards. Commissions are paid on the fifteenth of the month following the month in which the order was shipped. Commissions on all Christmas orders are paid December fifteenth
regardless of when the order was shipped. Thus commissions
are paid on all orders generally before we've received payment

from the account. If the billing has not been paid in ninety days, then the commission is withdrawn from the rep (deducted from his upcoming payment). Ultimately, the rep receives no commissions for sales to stores that do not pay their bills. It is to his advantage to be helpful in determining the creditability of an account.

We (and particularly Melvin) have worked long and hard to develop our relationships with the reps. We now have seventeen firms with sixty-five salespeople selling our cards in the United States and Canada. The firms represent us at each of the major gift or stationery shows, and Melvin spends much of his time traveling to these shows and getting to know most of these sixty-five people. Periodically we send newsletters to everyone, including information on new cards, new pricing and terms, the plans and progress of our company, well-known stores that are carrying and doing well with our cards, sales tips, advice and leads, and a good dose of friendliness. We go out of our way to make things easy for them, sending them samples and catalogs, encouraging them to call us collect if they have any questions or needs. They're the ones in the position to really make our business take off, so we have to keep on them, developing that relationship. Yet they hardly mind our harping on them if our cards are doing well—it's their steady source of income. A mutually beneficial relationship.

Our advertising expenditures and general efforts to stay directly in touch with stores have continued, although most of our orders now come through our reps. We provide the reps with catalogs, price sheets, and order forms (if they want them, although most use their own). Yet annually we'll send our catalogs, pricing information, and a list of reps directly to the stores, encouraging them to order in whatever way is convenient for them. The reps receive the commission even if the store orders directly from us. Unfair? No, not really. Again, you need the long-term perspective. If the reps are making some additional money off your line and see that the orders are rolling in—that it's easy to sell your products—then they are encouraged to work that much harder for you. When they see the potential return, they go for it. And everyone benefits in the long run.

Our sales are going very well. In 1978, we grossed $95,000. In 1979, we topped $300,000. We're hard at work expanding our product line: creating new card ideas and inscriptions, then completing the artwork and moving on to production, shipping, billing, etc. There's no end to it—it's largely a question of how far we want to take it. And at this point we're eager to take it quite a bit further.

In the fall of 1970, Susan Riecken went shopping for a new calendar and couldn't find anything she really liked. She had a pretty good idea of what she was after, and with the prospect of Christmas looming over her she decided to make one for herself and a couple extra to give as presents. "I took the original to a copy shop to be xeroxed," she remembers, "and they told me the reproductions would be better if I printed it offset. I said that would be fine, could I have five copies please? They explained that their minimum offset run was twenty-five. So I got twenty-five." Susan grins, only slightly ruefully. "I was really a babe in the woods. I've learned a lot in the last ten years."

She didn't know it at the time, but as she illustrated and assembled calendars at her kitchen table, Riecken was starting a business. Her tenth calendar was published two summers ago. *A Book for 1980* was produced in an edition of 4,000, her largest run yet. Each book contains twenty-six hand-printed full-color illustrations accompanied by fragments from the likes of Whitman, Thoreau, and Shakespeare. The little books sell very well indeed for $8.50 retail. "That's about medium price for engagement calendars," their designer says. But it's a real bargain for a bound portfolio of twenty-six monoprints, which is essentially what Susan Riecken creates.

Production of the calendars is labor intensive and time consuming. The type for the books is set with rubber stamps, each one designed by Riecken and hand-cut from rubber erasers. A master copy of the year's calendar, without illustrations, is off-set by a printer, but each of the illustrations is printed by hand, using special inks on blank stamp pads. With twenty-six illus-trations to a calendar and an edition of 4,000 calendars, that's a great deal of stamping. Although she hired an assistant to help with last summer's production, in previous years Riecken did everything herself, from designing and cutting the stamps to packaging and shipping the finished books. "For 1979 I did 3,500 books," she recalls, "and I discovered that 3,500 was absolutely the most I could do alone. It was not," she adds, "a pleasant experience."

Most new businesses don't spend much time worrying about expansion, but too much growth can present as many problems as too little. For Riecken, the rapid expansion of demand for her work has caused a continual evaluation of her goals and methods. The evolution of her calendar from a gift for friends to a business that could net her as much as $20,000 this year is a curious combination of intent and circumstance. It offers insight into the meandering path that a small business often takes.

With a $3,000 bank loan, Brook Jones took over a business in Waitsfield, Vermont, six years ago that produced about 3,000 specialized Christmas tree ornaments and had twenty-five wholesale customers. Since then, orders have nearly quintu-pled—most of the new business obtained through crafts shows and personal contacts.

Microcosmia, Inc., produces three basic ornaments, all of which are made in two-and-one-half-inch clear glass globes. The terrarium ornaments containing live plants in soil are the company's original product. Jones added a line of silk flower and dried flower ornaments.

Like other companies in Vermont and in other rural areas, Microcosmia uses a team of contract workers. In this case, Jones supplies seven persons with glass globes and tweezers and trains them in the art of ornament construction. Working primarily from August to December, they turn out anywhere from a couple of dozen to several hundred a week and are paid $3.50 to $9.00 for each dozen.

Ornaments sell at $30 per dozen wholesale to shopowners who get $5 to $7 each for them. Return on sales hase been sufficient to finance each succeedings year's production. The original loan has been paid off, and Microcosmia, Inc., is a totally self-financing and growing concern.

The Animal Town Game Company is a family effort headed by Jan and Ken Kolsbun with invaluable help from their young daughters Holly, Tuesday, and Dawn. The Kolsbuns, of Santa Barbara, California, design and manufacture family games.

Their games differ markedly from the giants of the field by dealing mostly with natural resources: bees, food production, whales, and water resources. Usually the purpose of the games is to teach players to save resources, not destroy or "develop" them, and often to work in cooperation rather than competition with game partners. The latest game, Madison Avenue–Reverse-It, contrasts giant advertising agency methods with those of Briarpatch businesses.

Annual sales have steadily risen from the $3,000 level of 1977. In 1978, sales were $18,000; in 1979, $46,000; and in 1980, $60,000. The mailing list is now computerized and has tripled to 15,000.

"All the big guys are going down," says Ken, "but we're going up in our fifth year. We're beginning to relax about the money end of things."

How do you market home-produced games in competition with major producers and distributors? In their old yellow van, the Kolsbuns visit an average of more than two arts, crafts, and energy fairs a month and set up their portable booth. "From 50,000 to 100,000 people show up on a weekend," Ken said, "so we come in front of a lot of people. And the word gets around. We also sell in a small number of stores that are interested in social and environmental issues. And we have a mail order system. We'll send out 14,000 catalogs this year in time for Christmas." And Christmas is indeed Santa Claus. About eighty percent of sales come in the last quarter of the year. The Kolsbuns' chief outlet for that season is the Yes store, a Santa Barbara arts and handicrafts mart that opens only for Christmas business. It grosses the Kolsbun game company $5,000 or more each holiday season. For year-round sales, the games sell best at the fairs near small mountain communities where the people have returned to the land, to the rural areas.

After all that, does it provide a living? Eventually, yes. But you lose some before you gain. Jan works as an electrocardiogram technician for a Santa Barbara hospital and is on call twenty-four hours via a radio receiver in her purse. It helps pay the way. Ken is an educated and experienced landscape and park planner, but he gives all his time now to the game company.

To get started, the Kolsbuns upped the mortgage on the house they bought before Santa Barbara real estate prices went crazy. They were turned down for loans at seven or eight banks that found the project completely outside the experience of conventional lending institutions. Then a new bank came to town, looking for business. That loan, together with savings of their own, got the Kolsbuns going on the first game in 1975.

"We grossed $500 in 1976 on our bee game, the Nectar Collector," Ken said. "The farm game the next year grossed us $7,500, and the whale game last year grossed $35,000, for a net of $6,000 in 1978. We are now ahead of last year's pace, and we have a good inventory on hand."

Are the conventional lending institutions now ready to grant the necessary financing? "I'm not interested in the banks anymore," Ken said. "I'll borrow from willing friends who grant low or no-interest loans. I usually pay them back in six months, but if I need more time I'm not under the pressure of a big bank."

The Kolsbuns are not trying to underprice the major producers. Their games sell for eleven or twelve dollars, except the whale game priced at seventeen dollars. "We are building respect into the games, together with quality, so that they'll last and not be thrown out after a few weeks," Ken said. "We don't want them to be a wasted resource. The whale game, our most expensive, is selling best because the pieces are made so well. It's not a schlock job."

If the games are based mostly on cooperation—if nobody wins and nobody loses, and you're not trying to beat somebody—where does the fun come in?

"We're not against competition per se," Ken replied. "We urge players to do their best. If you run a race, you should run it as fast as you can, but not with the idea of getting back at the other person. In our games you do the best you can but do not try to put down the other person. That's the difference between our concepts and the typical games in department stores."

Then there is competition in some of the games?

"There is a degree," Ken said, "as in our Back to the Farm game. You can play it two ways. You can be a very aggressive farmer, or you can be neighborly. The central theme is working through agricultural cooperatives, the small kind. And then, of course, there is the theme of cooperation with nature.

"Save the Whales is somewhat different. Players compete, but not against each other. They cooperate in a struggle against a system that in our minds represents many negative forces that are corrupting the world, from multinational corporations to bureaucratic organizations that are insensitive to the whale and the ecological system." Players try to avoid catcher ships, floating factories, oil spills, radioactive waste, and the International Whaling Commission. Whaling moratoriums and sanctuaries are sought, and sometimes storms and icebergs help by impeding the whaling ships. Also influencing the fate of the whales are the endangered species status, migration times and routes, and, finally, extinction of a species. "The only way you can 'win' this game is to save all eight whale species," the rulebook says. The game board is a colorful work of art, and the whales that move along the squares are silver-plated cast metal models of the eight species.

To develop their rules, the Kolsbuns put their games through a long, intensive test. "We play each game 100 or 200 times before we complete our rules," Ken said. "And that's where the daughters come in. They are really good critics, without realizing it."

A sixteen-dollar classified ad in *Workbench* magazine led thirty-one-year-old Dale Prohaska, Jr., into a mail-order toy business that grossed a quarter-million dollars in 1979. The ad offered "ten unique patterns for wooden toys for only $1."

Love-Built Toys & Crafts, Inc., of Tahoe City, California, began as a part-time business eight years ago with an initial outlay of fifty-five dollars for patterns. Consistent use of magazine ads and mail-order catalogs has resulted in sales of toy designs and basic parts throughout the United States, Mexico, and Canada, as well as in European countries. Purchasers include individuals, schools, craft shops, scouting organizations, and wholesalers.

A former schoolteacher, Prohaska became involved in toy construction in 1972, when he bought a wooden log toy truck for his six-month-old son. Figuring he could make a better one, he developed other wooden "toddler-proof" toys that could be made by home craftspersons with hand tools, without nails or screws. As orders increased, Prohaska eventually quit his elementary teaching position, rented a store where he designed wheeled wooden toys, and started his mail-order business for the patterns.

"The business plan for Love-Built Toys," Prohaska explains, "has changed from one of 'making it big' in the mail-order market to directing our major emphasis toward the wholesale market." By many standards, the growth of Love-Built has been impressive, but Prohaska adds: "Building a business that started with a $1,000 loan has not been without problems. Earlier this year, I changed the company structure from a sole proprietorship to a corporation because of the additional liability protection and also because it would be easier to grow financially."

Nestled in the heart of historic Georgetown in Washington, D.C., the Red Balloon is a refreshing alternative to the super-market-like toy emporiums sprouting up all over American suburbia. Proprietors Bob and Linda Joy opened their toy store nine years ago, after a five-year stint in the Peace Corps. While toys have changed a great deal in the last ten years, the philosophy behind the Red Balloon hasn't. "We decided we wanted to go into the toy business with the concept of finding the best things that we could for kids, be they toys, tools, science objects, or whatever. We wanted the safest and most interesting toys we could find, in terms of design and value. And we still follow basically the same premise today."

So the Red Balloon is stocked with everything from the traditional standbys to solar energy inventor kits and a sprawling menagerie of stuffed animals. There is an absence of TV-hyped gadgets, video games, mechanical sharks, and laser pistols.

The Joys moved the Red Balloon into its present high traffic location four years ago. The original location was about 200 square feet, posing problems for adequate storage and office space. The current building, in the same neighborhood, has about 850 square feet for retail space, plus about twice that amount for storing a huge inventory of items from around the world.

Bob believes his Peace Corps background has been "much, much more important" than a business degree. He journeyed to fifty-five countries in those five years and got "invaluable experience" from "just traveling around and seeing what other people do, what other cultures are like, walking around stores in other countries."

And Linda's experience from seven years of high-school teaching is evident as well. Often at the Red Balloon she is more a counselor to parents and a comforter to children than a shopkeeper. And that's just the way she likes it. With two young children, ages two and five, the Joys' experiences as parents are helpful to their customers—and, of course, to the ultimate recipients of the toys.

From its beginnings ten years ago, the Red Balloon has come a long way. Bob remembers that in the store's first two years, he worked construction jobs to augment the family income. "But now we own our own building, and the business is doing well."

HUMAN-SCALE SHOPS AND
CENTER CITY DEVELOPMENT

Carol Levitt's Craftworks in Frederick, Maryland, is an indoor, human-scale shopping center for antiques, crafts, collectibles, and the like. Since 1977, the Craftworks has offered space for businesspeople to display wares to the public; centralized cash register and receipts management; someone to answer phones, wait on customers, and make sales during working hours—all at extremely low cost and with minimum demands on the owner or the shopkeeper. The Craftworks gives new start-ups the opportunity to switch smoothly from their nonbusiness jobs, careers, and avocations to the reality of being in business.

"A lot of the people who get into this business," says Levitt, a portrait painter by training and inclination, "just don't really know if they can make it at this. They have an idea that maybe they could have a shop. It's that vague. We give them a chance to test their ideas, to get their feet wet."

A dozen budding businesspeople now operate tiny shops in

Index

Index

the Craftworks, which once was two large, vacant storefronts and a warehouse on Frederick's main shopping street, with a cavernous warehouse behind. A space about ten feet by ten feet is typical for the shops. That's just enough to set up a decent display and have room for a customer to move around a bit and browse. For that space, Levitt charges the shopkeeper fifty-five dollars a month. In some cases she reduces the rent in exchange for bartered goods or time manning the shop and tending the register at the front of the store, an arrangement she has with Catherine High, a shopkeeper selling collectibles, and Margaret Rattie, who sells knitting goods. The hours at the Craftworks are eleven to five, Wednesday through Sunday.

All sales flow through the central register, and the Craftworks takes ten percent off the top of all receipts. Together with rental and the commission, the Craftworks manages to meet its expenses and keep in business. The total retail operations gross something around $30,000 a year. Is the Craftworks making money? "Just barely," says Levitt. Is it making enough to pay her for the time and effort she puts into management, promotion, and tender loving care? "Not even close yet."

Sharing one of the two storefronts of the Craftworks is another Levitt enterprise run by Carol's husband Neil, a government scientist. The handcrafted stained glass sign in the window proclaims its name and function: The Deli. This small restaurant specializes in luncheon fare—unusual and tasty sandwiches and salads. Owned jointly by Neil and Philip Hiteshew, the Deli is making more money than the Craftworks, although daily operating expenses are much higher.

The Deli and the Craftworks exist in a symbiotic relationship. Each depends upon, and each helps, the other. Visitors to the Deli frequently end up in the Craftworks, and Craftworks customers often find themselves lunching in the Deli. Hanging on the walls of the Deli diningroom are castings from an old metal foundry—wheels, gears, and dogs—collectibles on consignment and for sale in the Craftworks. The

Deli's chairs—sturdy wooden peices bought at auction from the nearby Hood College cafeteria—have been hand-decorated with wood burned flowers by a Craftworks person. The Deli's stained glass sign was done by an artist who sold her glass work in the Craftworks.

All things considered, the Craftworks and the Deli may well be a unique case of how a person can go into business by helping others go into business.

Fifteen years ago, Philadelphia's South Street was a doomed thoroughfare with abandoned stores and sure signs of urban blight. Now it's a thriving commercial district, especially the four-block strip from Second to Sixth streets, with hundreds of small, privately owned shops. "People who come down to the area who haven't seen it in ten years," says Julia Zagar, who owns the Eyes Gallery with her husband Isaiah, "will exclaim, 'It's a miracle!' "

The miracle can be traced to the efforts of many individuals. Back in 1965, John and Sally Bos were scouting around for a low-rent district in which to open a repertory playhouse. Their Theater of the Living Arts (TLA), set up in an old movie house on the 300 block of South Street, was one of the few places offering top-flight drama in Philadelphia at the time. In spite of the location, it drew large audiences, mostly young people, and provided jobs for almost one hundred actors, set designers, technicians, and others, most of whom were graduates of one of the five art schools in the area. Taking up residence near the theater at rock-bottom rents, the people associated with TLA became the foundation for all that happened in the ensuing years to make South Street come alive again.

In 1968, when TLA was in its third season, the Zagars, just out of the Peace Corps, were looking for a location to open a gallery and crafts shop. Having trained Peruvians in the production of jewelry, sculpture, baskets, and woven clothing, they had returned to the United States with crates full of these wares, eager to sell them.

Aside from their Peace Corps savings, the only capital they had at the time was the stock of goods they had brought back with them from Peru. They did not need much more. John and Sally Bos put them in touch with a man who owned a building down the street and who was willing to let them rent all three floors—about 1,500 square feet—for seventy-five dollars a month. Settling in on the upper floors, the Zagars put a few coats of paint on the old storefront and cleaned up the shop. The Eyes Gallery opened for business.

At first, the Zagars were only open when TLA had a show on. "We would run out to catch people when the show was over to get them to come over to the shop," Julia recalls. What little government aid flowed into South Street came indirectly that first winter: The Zagars needed food stamps to get by. "It was a struggle," says Julia, "but our needs were simple then."

The following summer the Zagars helped organize a weekend open air crafts market at Head House Square, a small but popular commercial block at the edge of Society Hill. The crafts fair was a major success, and word of the Eyes Gallery and its unique merchandise began to spread. That fall, with enough confidence in the future of their business and a growing conviction that somehow South Street itself had a future, the Zagars invested their life savings and money borrowed from their parents to buy their building outright for $10,000. The property is now worth twenty times that amount. And anyone renting the store alone would have to pay about $1,000 a month.

By 1970 several other entrepreneurs had recognized the opportunity South Street presented. Most were young, in their twenties or thirties, and nearly all were in some way connected with the art world. A twenty-nine-year-old woodcarver began selling fine furniture crafted in his own shop. Another young man put a mere $500 into opening a store to sell handmade jewelry, and another couple created and sold metal sculpture made from recycled junk.

Among the newcomers were Rick and Ruth Snyderman, who opened the Works art gallery in 1970. They soon joined the Zagars and a few others as community leaders whose vision and energy galvanized the area's residents into an active battle against the city and the state to prevent construction of a proposed expressway. Forming the South Street Renaissance, a community and business association, they struck up alliances with other neighborhood groups. Several members of the Renaissance knowledgeable in media manipulation got local newspapers and television stations to pay more attention to the environmental and social issues raised by the proposed highway. Persistent well-organized demonstrations and presentations at public hearings resulted in success for South Street. By 1973 the crosstown expressway was dead. Later in the year the Renaissance group forced a change in the planned exit ramps on Interstate I-95 that had also threatened the community.

Even before these victories the street had flourished. Promotional campaigns such as "Hippy House Tours" had exploited the residents' unusual life styles and they had been good for business. More significant still was the South Street restaurant boom. In 1970, the thirteen founders of the Renaissance had contributed fifty dollars apiece to start a cafe called the Crooked Mirror. Run by local artists, it made every dish a masterpiece of color, texture, and flavor. The manager of the coffeehouse and two of the cooks then started their own restaurant, the Black Banana, and launched the Philadelphia restaurant boom. Three other similar restaurants soon opened in the area, all successful ventures and all run by artists.

When the Black Banana first opened, it paid one hundred dollars a month rent. To get going, it relied on one of the mainstays of South Street: cooperative assistance. Most of the people in the small community were willing to help each other out, scraping old paint, sanding, painting, doing construction. Several of the struggling artists developed professional skills in plumbing, carpentry, and electrical work, later going into business as contractors. In any case, the city did not bother sending building code inspectors to check on things. "I think the best thing the city did for South Street was to leave it alone," says Julia Zagar. "They figured it was all going to become a highway anyway."

Until the expressway battles were over, business grew but remained modest. Many shops were open on erratic schedules, and store fixtures were often minimal and recycled. People were there as much for the camaraderie as for the desire to make money. "The people here had very strong ideas about urban life," Rick Snyderman declares. "They wanted to make the street a haven for intellectual and cultural exchange. That was their marketplace. South Street was as much a cultural marketplace as a commercial marketplace."

By 1974, when the highway was no longer a threat, things were changing rapidly. "Many of us recognized at this point that there was a golden opportunity here on South Street that would last for a limited time," says Snyderman, one of the few South Street newcomers who had previous business experience. When he and Ruth opened the Works he had a dozen years behind him in his family's finance company. "We urged many of our friends to buy their buildings if at all possible." Many did, thanks in large part to the opening of a new branch of a local bank just a few blocks away in Society Hill. The branch began soliciting accounts, and with the highway problems behind them the South Street merchants were able to secure mortgages and business loans. Within a year, the real estate market had already revived remarkably, and by early 1975 the bargains were gone. A corner building available for $7,500 in early 1974 sold for $40,000 by the end of the same year.

As rents rose sharply, some businesses without long-term leases went under, as did those that were poorly managed or severely undercapitalized. Others branched out to become more profitable. Rosebud, for instance, a store selling second-hand clothing, began manufacturing denim wear, t-shirts, sweatshirts, and silk-screened and hand-painted clothing. With three or four years of retailing experience, merchants able to demonstrate a plan for expansion were able to get the necessary financing. Some, with unusual businesses and fiercely loyal clientele, had customers who offered to be "angels" and provide discount rate loans. One couple volunteered to finance one of the Zagars' annual buying expeditions to South America. Other businesses received loans from some of the older, established merchants on the street who had managed to hang on.

Few stores remain vacant on South Street today. The merchants have prospered, although none has reaped extravagant fortunes (aside from the windfall rise in the value of their properties). Ed Stein of Stein's Dinette Center, the first non-arts-related business to come into the area after the revival, has had increased sales every year since he opened in 1974, contrary to industry trends. One of the oldest businesses on the street, Auerbach's, which sells children's clothing and grossed a respectable $500,000 in 1970, does about forty percent better than that today. On the other hand, Julia Zagar notes that she knows other people in her line of business who do far more than her $150,000 a year in sales, but she feels that the advantages of living on South Street are a priceless compensation. Her costs are lower than those in a mall or in a more traditional commercial district.

"There's a real compulsion about South Street that seems to hold people here," Rick Snyderman notes. "They love it." Indeed, it offers one of the few opportunities for businesspeople to live and work in a personally rewarding environment. The community, now numbering over 1,500, is too large to be one big happy family, but the sense of togetherness remains strong.

Naturally, the area has its problems. Teenagers hang out on the street on weekend nights, occasionally disturbing shoppers. Litter is a major nuisance, but in typical South Street fashion merchants have collectively hired some of the area young people to sweep up on Saturday and Sunday mornings.

That same cooperative spirit was responsible for the planting of curbside trees on two blocks of the strip. After a resident (whose brother-in-law worked in the city Park Department) made arrangements for the delivery of the trees South Streeters had petitioned for, half a dozen shopowners organized a weekend digging and planting party.

The biggest problem is a lack of parking spaces. The city commissioned a feasibility study for a parking lot at Fifth and South streets, but nothing has been done. There may soon be a solution to the problem, though, because the entire east side of the city suffers from the same shortage. "God," exclaims Ed Stein, "if we only had adequate parking down here, who knows what would happen?"

In the fall of 1975, New York City announced overall cutbacks in day care as part of its austerity program. The Queens neighborhood in which Linda Hazel lived, comprised mostly of black families with working mothers, was particularly hard hit. A city day care director with twenty years' experience operating programs, Hazel's simmering anger at the city's neglectful attitude came to a full boil.

"If you spend the proper amount of money on children between the ages of eight months and six years you'll save billions on the other end," argued Hazel, who holds a master's degree in early childhood education. "And if you take children out of day care, viably employed parents would have to quit their jobs. Being black, I just didn't appreciate it. You tell people to take destiny over their own lives yet, good lord, every time they make a move they get banged on the head."

Determined to start her own neighborhood day care center, Hazel began looking for funding, only to discover that most sources were dry. "It was particularly hard being a minority woman in a redlined area in a city that wasn't lending," she explained. She went to the Small Business Administration, but their advisors viewed her plan as a service, not a business. She applied to foundations but had no luck. Finally, she and her partner Antoinette Everette went to the community. The homeowners recognized that Hazel's idea met their needs, and in two months she raised $12,500. It was enough for a down payment on a recently closed nursing home, a sprawling thirty-two room complex.

"Everything was an attempt to stay in business," reminisced the thirty-eight-year-old director, sitting in her office. They sold the hospital beds that had come with the nursing home. They held cake sales, took in children on weekends, rented out some of the rooms as office space, bought supplies at a flea market, and moved into apartments they made in the attic.

"I had the technical knowledge from working with the city. I can make up budgets, but that's not what it is," Hazel stressed. A sing-song alphabet drifted in from the classroom down the hall. "When you know every dime collected means whether or not you'll operate, everything changes. We had to forget our social service orientation and start dealing with business as business."

Today, A Betterway cares for fifty youngsters, aged six months to six years. Last year, the school, which charges $38 to $45 a week per child, grossed $100,000. "It's taken three years to meet a three-month projection," Hazel said. "We're just now seeing black ink."

"There is a tremendous pent-up demand for durables," the co-owner of a California garden tools company told me recently. "We are and have been constantly behind on orders for six months because we have not been able to anticipate demand."

And, as the businesses just described indicate, there is a pent-up demand for lasting goods and quality services of all kinds. The businesses that have sprung up to satisfy this demand come in all varieties: home-based, retail, mail order, on-the-farm, and center-city. The spirit and results of this new small business movement are evident everywhere these days, and the fact that increasing numbers of college students are starting service businesses is a strong indication that this movement has just begun to grow.

4

Sideline Enterprises

"I'm fifty-eight years old, and I plan to retire in seven years, but I don't want to sit around watching TV. And I'll need extra income to keep ahead of inflation. That's why I'm testing different ways to get into the mail-order business." The person who spoke those words is a mechanical engineer with our local power company—not exactly the type usually envisioned to plan such a venture. In his particular case, though, the mail-order idea came from his daughter, who is a marketing manager for a direct response company. Predictably, he was using his organized engineering approach to investigate the products that reflected both his interests and the marketplace.

A few days later, another neighbor about the same age told us of his retirement plans that began with a sideline accounting service. Given the opportunity for early retirement, he had clear plans for building up part-time income working on bookkeeping and financial services for small businesses in our area.

73

For hundreds of thousands of persons facing retirement who are taking steps toward their own business, sideline enterprises are a constructive path to fighting inflation and enjoying freedom from corporate environs. We're continually hearing from people in their fifties and sixties who are using their basement, spare room, garage, or rented space to develop an income-producing activity.

These efforts are not restricted to preretirement individuals either. As mentioned in the last chapter, many college students have developed small businesses on the side while attending classes. For a great many individuals with entrepreneurial desires, sidelining makes the most sense in terms of financing, experience, risk balancing, peace of mind, and future success. It takes time to learn when to take the big risk—and the more knowledge you acquire while investments are modest, the better your chances for future success can be.

Some individuals use a combination of several sidelines to make up a full line. On a farm tucked away in the New Hampshire mountains, Allan Block earns his income (and satisfaction) as a craftsman, poet, farmer, and fiddler. Block moved his leather workshop from New York City about ten years ago to a farm near Peterborough where he spends several hours a day making leather sandals, handbags, and belts. By fulfilling the demand that he has created for his leatherwork, Block is able to generate enough cash flow to support him in his other endeavors and hobbies.

An enterprising person, Block keeps copies of his latest collection of poems available at his shop, as well as his new recording—an album of fiddle and square dancing music.

Even a field like energy development is open for sidelining. David Blume founded American Homegrown Fuel Company in San Francisco with the concept of making alcohol fuel from garbage and other organic wastes. Blume teaches people attending his Homegrown Fuel seminars to make a "column still," a 300-gallon tank set on top of a fire box and topped off by three-meter condensing pipes. Blume maintains that converting a car to use alcohol fuel can be done for about thirty dollars in two or three hours with some drill bits, a pair of pliers, and a diagram of the car's carburetor.

Another California company—this one farther south in Manhattan Beach—is also shoestringing an energy business based on alcohol fuels. Terry Spragg of Solargas Corporation sells a system—including a holding tank for the mash—for about $500 to produce five to fifteen gallons of alcohol a day. The key to his system is reported to be a patented distillation column that creates a vacuum, thereby reducing the boiling point of alcohol from 174 to 120 degrees Fahrenheit. A conventional solar heating device can produce that temperature.

Others, using similar sideline approaches, are looking at ways to create another energy source, methane, from materials that range from manure to paper and food wastes. Sideline businesses have become widespread in the solar, wood stove, chimney sweeping, wind, and energy conservation fields.

"Starting Up for Under $500" was the title of an *In Business* article by Michael Ketcher, who described how several persons in the San Francisco Bay area developed sidelines on a shoestring. "The complete meal for today's warrior" is the line Joseph Nixdorf of Berkeley uses to sell his meatless, dairyless, burrito-shaped sandwich called the Samurai Hero. Nixdorf started the business two years ago, after several years of studying macrobiotic cooking. His only initial expenses—less than fifty dollars—were for a stainless steel pot and for the ingredients: chapati, brown rice, tofu, tahini, soy sauce, and various vegetables.

He made the first batch of about sixty sandwiches in his kitchen, loaded them on his bicycle, and pedaled them around to the natural food stores in his community hoping eventually to build a regular clientele. Nixdorf originally delivered sandwiches to customers five days a week but found that they were as fresh the second day as the first. He pared his work week down to three days, making deliveries on Monday, Wednesday, and Friday.

Recently, Nixdorf hired two people part time to help him wrap, but to insure the correct balance of ingredients he still makes the sandwiches himself. His other major expense is seventy-five dollars a month for shared warehouse space.

The retail price for the Samurai Hero is $1.88 to $2.00; wholesale price, $1.50; and cost of making the sandwich, about $.80. Nine stores carry the hero, mostly health food stores. Nixdorf is considering expanding to other outlets, such as the food carts that abound near the University of California campus and mobile snack trucks.

Carl Levinson provides another example of starting a sideline business with a minimum of capital. You can hardly go into a laundromat or supermarket in San Francisco without seeing one of his flyers on the bulletin board advertising his class, "Creative Cooking for Singles." By day Levinson is a psychotherapist with a private practice and a teacher of dream therapy at the University of San Francisco. But three nights a week his apartment becomes a classroom, where he unveils his recipes for Chicken Cubano, Stewed Beef in Wine Sauce with Star Anise, Omelettes Continental, and other gourmet dishes.

Levinson started with about $200. First he registered with City Hall and got a business license. He called it the San Francisco Cultural Institute, a name broad enough to cover any other activities he might want to start, such as a film series or courses in other subjects. Levinson has already added two additional cooking classes.

Advertising flyers, posted on bulletin boards and distributed in San Francisco's financial district, bring in most of Levinson's customers. He cuts costs by writing, laying out, and distributing the flyers himself, and he buys his equipment, such as pots, pans, and silverware, at discount stores or restaurant supply houses. The registration fee for the four session course is twenty dollars, and each one may have as many as twenty students. A small additional food fee is required for each class session. The menu changes every month to give students a chance to learn new dishes and to encourage repeat business.

"Some of the happiest retired couples I know started an antique business on the side some years back," Don Cunnion of Harleysville, Pennsylvania, maintains. Cunnion has been making surveys of the array of businesses started as a part-time or "moonlighting" effort. Some refer to them as kitchen businesses. "The great thing about the antique business is that it combines travel and people contact—two qualities most older persons particularly enjoy."

Bill Highouse of southeastern Pennsylvania got into locksmithing as a sideline. He began with a few hundred dollars' worth of equipment, traveling from job to job in his station wagon. Now, his business established, he operates out of a rolling shop—a van complete with key machines, drills, and replacement locks. The entire set-up cost him $16,000, including a special generator that supplies current for electrically operated equipment.

Sideline commercial efforts are extremely prevalent in the crafts field. Magazines such as *Fibre Arts, Crafts Report,* and *Creative Crafts* regularly report such activities. Often craftspeople join together in a cooperative marketing effort. Five weavers working in partnership near South Penobscot, Maine, are successfully producing and marketing a line of handwoven clothing: tunics and tabards, shawls, skirts, caftans, jackets, and capes. After three years, North Country Textiles has annual sales of more than $40,000, and they are steadily expanding, according to the *Crafts Report.* Each weaver has a specific responsibility in addition to producing fabric. Carole Ann Larson writes orders and handles shipping as well as the bookkeeping. Sheila Denny-Brown and June Sproule concentrate on sales and marketing. Ron King works on the design of the garments—fabrics, sizing, and tailoring. Georgia Beatty is the secretary. In addition, there's usually an apprentice weaver.

The weavers work in their own homes, use their own equipment, and are paid by the piece. Currently, they earn over four dollars per hour. The partners work out the budget, calculating the cost for each item, then marking up eighty percent for the wholesale price. Generally the retail price is double that, and items are sold in the showroom at a slight discount. Close to seventy-five percent of their sales are wholesale, with most of the sales contacts generated through the American Craft Enterprises markets in Rhinebeck, New York, and Baltimore.

An example of "high technology" in a home-based business is provided by David and Roberta Crocker in their suburban neighborhood in Needham, Massachusetts. In the living room, for instance, a considerable space has been given over to an imposing orange and tan piece of electronic office equipment, sporting a keyboard and video display terminal. Reports J. Tevere MacFadyen:

> That's the Crockers' Addressograph-Multigraph Comp/Set 500 phototypesetting machine.
> There is another just like it, only newer and bigger, close by in what seems once to have been the Crockers' den but is now a room devoted to their extensive collection of graphic design tools and materials: a light table and waxer, a deeply piled desk and a transmission densitometer, and a storage for a variety of other items. There's no ping-pong table in the Crockers' cellar. Instead, it boasts complete darkroom facilities, a formidable NuArc copy camera, a vacuum frame and art lamp, a PMT (photo-mechanical transfer) processor for making instant photostats, as well as small letterpress and more storage.
> Upstairs, now that the kids have grown and moved away from home, their rooms too have succumbed to the tide of sophisticated hardware, filling inevitably with keyboards and consoles.

The equipment in their home comprises an efficient, highly flexible typesetting and word processing system. Crockergraphics handles everything from campaign buttons for local candidates to city street directories. For some clients, often area printers or publishers, the Crockers will do complete design, layout, typesetting, and paste-up. For others, they might generate computer-printed mailing labels from a supplied address list. Still others, like the students from two nearby high schools, have been trained by the Crockers and simply rent machine time to do their own work (in the case of the students, preparation of school newspapers). Telephone link-ups between Crockergraphics' computer facility and their clients' machines allows the direct transmission of copy, such as the lengthy contents of Wellesley College's alumnae directory, so that it can be processed and typeset without having to be laboriously keyboarded all over again.

None of this would seem especially remarkable if David Crocker were a printer or typesetter by trade, but he's not. He's a computation specialist employed full time by the Charles Stark Draper Laboratory in Cambridge (formerly a research component of MIT, where he received his degree in electrical engineering). An operation that has expanded until it's almost taken over his home is the ultimate result of something begun, innocently enough, as a pastime. "We got started in printing, purely as a hobby, right after Christmas in 1959. We were looking for something fun for the two of us to do together. If there was any financial motivation at all, it was to have the hobby pay for itself." Today, the Crockers' hobby pays for itself and then some. Crockergraphics last year grossed approximately $80,000. Figures for the third quarter of 1980 show a jump in earnings of almost fifty percent, with this year's anticipated gross now projected at better than $110,000.

Concludes journalist MacFadyen in his report on this example of high technology's role in a "cottage industry":

Clearly, Crockergraphics has outgrown its recreational status; but it's worth noting that though Roberta works full time at it and David allots the bulk of his off hours to the endeavor, neither is quite willing to relinquish their original aims. In important ways their business remains what it once was, something fun for them to do together, and its operating philosophy clings to that principle. "Some people like to go out and play golf on a Saturday," David remarks. "I like to be here, tinkering with this stuff." Scheduling is kept deliberately flexible, allowing both principals to pursue diverse activities elsewhere. Work on Crockergraphics projects is frequently reserved for late evenings when David is home from the lab. "I'll often be listening to the eleven o'clock news on TV while we finish up," Roberta notes. "It's definitely more than a part-time job," David grants, "and yet it's somehow different from a job. We have more control. When something comes up that we want to do, we do it. Besides, we really like doing this." In this light the presence of word processing and typesetting equipment all over their house doesn't seem so strange, because it makes possible the integration of home, hobby, and livelihood that Crockergraphics exemplifies.

5

Appropriate Technology as Small Business

Over the past ten years, increasing attention has been focused on "appropriate technology" in such areas as energy, agriculture, housing, waste management, communications, and health. Much of the attention came about following publication of *Small Is Beautiful: Economics As If People Mattered* (Harper & Row, 1973) by E. F. Schumacher. The British economist explored the need for new technologies, especially in developing nations, that would enhance community development and be compatible with the human and capital resources that were available locally and that would relate to the area's environmental needs.

Appropriate technology (AT) has become an umbrella for a wide range of thought and actions, mostly personal, but increasingly commercial in expression. By June 1978, it had even manifested itself in the U.S. Congress when a group of senators and representatives requested an exploratory study on AT by the Office of Technology Assessment (OTA). As part of that study, five criteria were identified: technical, social, environmental, economic, and financial. "Basic to AT perspectives," wrote Wade Greene, a critic of modern "progress," "is the notion that large-scale technology can be destructive not only to the environment but also to the human psyche. Thus, the challenge, as AT enthusiasts see it, is nothing less than reorienting human attitudes."

And the enthusiasts, like AT itself, cover a wide spectrum. According to the OTA draft report, they include do-it-yourselfers in New Mexico, back-to-the-woods homesteaders in Missouri, environmentalists in Washington state, 1960s social activists in Massachusetts, farmers in Nebraska, old-line socialists and new wave co-opers in New York City, academics in California, and antipoverty workers and antigovernment conservatives in Wyoming. More and more, their ranks are being swelled by businesspeople aware of resource constraints that translate into higher costs of doing business and the consequent need for alternatives.

"What is common," noted the OTA study, "is a strong desire for greater self-reliance, less dependence on government, and freedom from domination by big utilities and corporations. It is a movement to regain a measure of lost control and autonomy—control over vital aspects of living, such as food production and home energy, and autonomy in the sense of reduced dependence on large organizations."

Clearly, America's new business movement is made up of many people who fully appreciate the need for appropriate technologies of all kinds. These men and women are "entrepreneuring for the future" as they develop businesses in solar energy, compost toilets, methane fuels, resource recovery, wind machines, and biological agriculture. They are leading the way to what Hazel Henderson refers to as a "new economy of permanence which will require much technological innovation. Many such new technologies are most efficient if they are decentralized. They will therefore foster a vast new generation of inventors and small businesses."

This chapter profiles a few of the persons we have come

across who are using appropriate technologies to develop their own small businesses.

INTEGRATED PEST MANAGEMENT

While U.S. farmers are spraying over one billion pounds of pesticide annually, the Rincon-Vitova Insectaries, Inc., is raising a crop of billions of pest-consuming beneficial insects. Most Rincon-Vitova insects are sold to the emerging integrated pest management (IPM) industry. The IPM practitioner distributes the beneficial bugs among the farms using IPM. For Rincon-Vitova, the wholesale market far exceeds direct marketing to individual farmers and home gardeners.

Insectary partners Jack Blehm and Everett Dietrick grow and harvest the beneficial insects fifty miles north of Los Angeles in Ventura, California. The business started in 1960 after they met while doing fieldwork in Texas cotton. Dietrick had just completed a fifteen-year career as a research entomologist at the University of California when he was hired to do field research in Texas on the beneficial insect known as *Trichogramma.*

"Our big breakthrough came in 1962," Dietrick explained, "when a group of farmers from a cotton gin cooperative in California came to me and expressed interest in implementing an IPM program." The farmers had experienced the pesticide treadmill: rising pesticide use, increased insect control costs, and pesticide-induced insect outbreaks. These types of pesticide problems have induced many farmers to make the switch to IPM, which incorporates biological and cultural methods into the pest control program. Pesticides may still be used in an IPM program when needed. However, the ecologically unsound effects of chemicals are reduced to the absolute minimum.

"Our philosophy at the insectary is to help reduce pesticide use and minimize crop production costs," says Dietrick. "This involves releasing beneficial insects to augment the naturally occurring biological controls." The beneficial insects are best utilized within IPM programs that include regular crop monitoring.

Finding customers has been a word-of-mouth process. For example, the first big cotton IPM contract came about through a local friendship cultivated during Dietrick's days as a university researcher. Personal contacts are maintained with all the distributors and independent IPM practitioners who purchase insects. The partners make regular visits to Texas, Mexico, and Central America. On these trips, they dispense technical advice while firming up their personal relationships with customers.

The insects are shipped through the mails, which involves obtaining the necessary permits from the state and federal government agriculture departments. A copy of the necessary permit is pasted onto the shipping package along with the notice that this is a fragile package of live insects. During the hot summer months, insects must be shipped at night for early morning delivery. The postal service and most air freight services offer some type of overnight delivery.

"Weather is the number one factor affecting our markets," notes Blehm. Drought in Texas has reduced agricultural activity and limited beneficial insect sales. Floods have wiped out crops and reduced the market in Central America. Even political events can change the market. Since beneficial insects are a perishable commodity with a relatively short shelf-life (possibly one week), lessened demand from the markets means overproduction of insects that cannot be resold. Thus, an element of high risk is involved in raising beneficial insects.

Capital investment in the insectary has proceeded slowly over the last twenty years. Land, vehicles, buildings, microscopes, and insect-rearing equipment are all necessary. Recycling old railroad refrigerator cars for use as insectary buildings was cheaper than building structures from scratch. The old refrigerator cars are good for rearing insects because they are well insulated.

Rincon-Vitova raises several species of beneficial insects, but the pinhead size Trichogramma wasp is the most popular. Trichogramma wasps lay their eggs inside moth and butterfly eggs and thereby prevent the emergence of pestiferous worms and caterpillars. Insectary buildings are devoted to rearing moth eggs, which are then collected and pasted onto cardboard squares. (A one-inch cardboard square may hold 5,000 moth eggs.) The squares are then transferred to other buildings housing insect sting cages full of Trichogramma. The "stung" eggs are then shipped out and used by IPM practitioners because more Trichogramma will hatch out of the "stung" moth eggs. The rearing of the beneficial insects is the labor-intensive part of the operation. The insect cultures must be constantly watched and tended.

Organically grown grain—free of pesticides—is essential to rearing a crop of healthy moths for Trichogramma production. Scale insect parasites are raised on locally grown banana squash for use in citrus orchards. At any one time, the insectary may be raising a dozen or more different species of beneficial insects. Some beneficial insects, such as the green lacewing, eat a wide variety of pests; other beneficial insects may specialize in certain pests, such as California red scale in citrus or greenhouse whitefly.

Much of the technology used in raising beneficial insects has evolved from a learning-by-doing approach, although some of the basics are available in the scientific literature. It is recommended that someone entering this field first learn the basics from an established private enterprise or university. "Rincon-Vitova is inventing its own methods and machinery for doing the job better," says Jack Blehm.

SEWAGE DISPOSAL ALTERNATIVES

The compost toilet principle and the people who are in the business of marketing compost toilets exemplify appropriate technology and the challenge of developing an AT business.

The pioneer of the effort in the United States has been Abby Rockefeller, who heard about a Swedish unit called the Clivus Multrum, obtained rights to market it in North America, and then toiled away for a decade out of her company offices in Cambridge, Massachusetts. Her company is alive and well, and the job of developing a compost toilet industry now involves other dedicated and capable persons.

For years, rural communities have blindly endorsed the septic tank, and small towns have climbed just as blindly aboard the centralized sewage treatment bandwagon. Careful scrutiny of the appropriate use of a septic tank was rare, and careful analysis of the economics of sewage hook-ups was just as rare because the federal government paid for most of the town's share.

Michael Skenfield's professional involvement with water quality in mountain areas goes back over twenty years. National Forest management work introduced him to the effects that rural communities have on their watershed.

"The popular American toilet was using between 3.5 and 6 gallons of cold water to move a pint of fecal matter into a 1,000-gallon tank containing a liquid environment barely acceptable to its predatory inhabitants," says Skenfield, describing the conventional flush/septic tank system. He began researching alternatives for sewage disposal, and the compost toilet system looked worthwhile. "This method not only removed the water medium from the pathogens, but it plunked them right into the middle of the richest form of microbe rich topsoil. A system made to order!"

In the past four years, Skenfield, his wife Janet, and partner Tom Scheller in Murphys, California, have gained experience with the installation and use of commercial compost toilet systems—Clivus Multrum, Toa Throne, Carousel, Ecolet, and Bioloo. All originated in Sweden and were brought to America for distribution. Clivus Multrum, Toa Throne, and Carousel are considered "large composters" that can actually develop a heat-of-compost without an additional source. In these units, toilet wastes drop down a vertical, noncorrosive chute into an impervious tank partly filled with peat moss and garden top-soil. Small units like Ecolet and Bioloo sit on the bathroom floor; they make up for lack of storage capacity by providing electric heating surfaces beneath the tank to speed organic decomposition. All models, both large and small, are equipped with vent fans to draw air over the wastes and up the vent stack.

Skenfield's firm, Domestic Environmental Alternatives, introduced compost toilets to Calaveras County, California, through a close working relationship with a former county health officer and a number of enlightened clients. Most of their customer clients have thoroughly studied the compost toilet concept "and have already convinced themselves that they want one. What they need from me," says Skenfield, "is detailed location and installation advice, and lots of help toward getting their installation approved by their health department." He concludes: "Our time is coming! Saving energy is becoming a household phrase. We at DEA have laid the groundwork in our area. What we now need to do is to learn to run a business efficiently so that we can keep our costs down and concentrate on friendly, personal service."

We first met Heather Baldwin at the 1980 Composting and Waste Recycling Conference in Los Angeles. She and her husband started to market the Mullbank composting toilet out of their home in Campton, New Hampshire, five years before. Today their headquarters has been moved into a renovated outbuilding, their marketing and dealership techniques have become consistently sounder, and their product line has increased, but the business remains as personal and labor intensive as when it began. It's obviously hard work. For example, Heather brought along a Mullbank to exhibit at the Composting Conference and had to convince an airport porter that she wanted to take the toilet to the hotel despite his assurances that "every room in the hotel had its own bathroom."

Originally the Baldwins started selling compost toilets part time to keep busy in the summer and to generate extra income. "We found we enjoyed toilet selling more than teaching. We knew we couldn't do both full time, and toilets won out," explained Heather.

The first full year they had a dealership for Mullbank, they sold ten units but had no capital expense. When they sold one unit, they had the money to buy the next. "We had no formal business training or experience," recalls Heather, "but by the second year we had hired a high school girl to do our typing. We sold maybe thirty units that second summer. It was such a good summer for toilet sales that we hired a full time secretary."

To diversify their business, they branched out into water conservation devices and also began selling a pressurized, two-quart flush toilet, sold mainly for commercial installations where compost toilets can't be used. By the third year, more than 1,000 units had been sold.

The U.S. market has great potential for compost toilets, from the arid Southwest with its lack of water to the Northeast with its water pollution problems. "Five years ago, we were way ahead of our time. In another five to ten years, people will be forced to stop dumping; the country is beginning to wake up. We're very thankful we're not in the tourist trade. No matter what happens, people will always have to go to the bathroom," concludes Gunnar Baldwin.

Compost toilets are only one part of the "on-site wastewater" system being developed as alternatives to conventional centralized sewage treatment. In Boulder, Colorado, a company called PureCycle has developed a closed-loop system analogous in some ways to the sophisticated technology used in manned space flight. By 1980, four years after it was founded, PureCycle had revenues of $225,000, some twenty-five systems operating and another twenty in the process of installation. Within the next two years, the company forecasts sales of 1,000 units annually.

The totally contained household water recycling system uses microprocessor technology. The PureCycle System consists of three basic components: a 1,500-gallon tank to store incoming wastewater, a purification system operated and monitored by the microprocessor, and a 1,500-gallon cistern to store the purified water. The system is initially charged with a water supply of 1,500 gallons, to be used for all household purposes and eventually becoming wastewater. A series of purification and treatment processes then yields potable water again. Ultrafine membrane filters, activated carbon, and ion exchange resins remove organic contaminants and minerals. Final sterilization is provided by ultraviolet light. The entire process takes four hours. Water loss from the system is estimated at one percent. The system costs about $12,000 to install, and the company charges $33 per month for maintenance and service.

According to *Business Week,* the potential market for such systems is substantial. Thirty percent of U.S. homes—about 600,000 built each year—are not hooked up to central water and sewage systems. Warren Van Genderen, president of PureCycle, says, "Our figures show that in the United States each year, $800 million is spent for sites where you can't put in a septic tank or leach field."

The PureCycle technology illustrates the point that appropriate technology is by no means always simple technology.

Steve Serfling, president of Solar AquaSystems in Encinitas, California, and his colleagues developed the AquaCell Wastewater Treatment Process from their work with the cultivation of freshwater shrimp and fish in a closed system. After obtaining a patent for the AquaCell in 1973, Serfling and his partner, Dominick Mendola, pooled about $15,000 to set up a prototype for research and development. In 1976, Solar Aqua-Systems constructed a test wastewater unit to treat human sewage at the Cardiff, California, community plant.

The following year, the city of Hercules, California, contracted with the company for a feasibility study, and in 1980 the AquaCell system began full-scale operations. The Hercules system makes full use of the water hyacinth, which is an essential element in stabilizing the dissolved and suspended solids in the wastewaters treated at the plant.

Extensive studies have shown that the plants and animals used in the AquaCell process are generally hardy and able to withstand some fluctuations in nutrient content and air and water temperatures. A critical component of the system is the greenhouse cover, which allows solar energy and heat from the effluent wastewater, kept at fifty to sixty degrees Fahrenheit throughout the year, to be retained so that temperatures are kept at even levels throughout the day and from season to season. The AquaCell illustrates how complex and challenging an appropriate technology can be to implement and how important that implementation is to solving critical societal problems.

RECYCLING WASTES TO THE LAND

John O'Neal wanted to be a farmer, but he didn't have the land or the capital. His business—Ad+Soil—revolves around that desire to be a farmer.

After earning a master's degree at the University of Oklahoma in sanitary engineering, O'Neal spent three years in the regulatory office of the Environmental Protection Agency. Gradually he came to recognize "the cyclical system that some technology is trying to separate us from." Specifically, he became increasingly aware of what byproducts can do when recycled back to the land. More specifically, he decided to organize a company that would contract with cities and industries to apply their sludge to land—a direct method to recover nutrients that otherwise turn into pollutants.

Ad+Soil was formed in January 1979, and now employs eight professionals and ten nonprofessionals. The West Chester, Pennsylvania, company has contracts with Philadelphia and Battle Creek, Michigan, as well as with the Wyeth Pharmaceutical Company in West Chester.

Wilson Nolan's company—BioGro Systems of Annapolis, Maryland—started on a part-time basis in his kitchen. By the end of 1980, BioGro had fifty employees, annual sales of $2 million, offices in five states, and crews applying wastes to land from Maryland to Arkansas. Nolan now flies to job sites in his own company plane. Half of their clients are municipalities; the other half are companies in the food, paper, chemical, and textile fields.

Nolan credits his experience as a cook in the army with giving him just as valuable background for his present company as the master's degree in agronomy he received at the University of Arizona. The BioGro program for land application of sludge consists of these major functions: (1) preparing program planning and analysis reports; (2) obtaining land applications sites and permits; (3) supplying transport fleet tankers, land applicators and pumps; (4) directing the complete program management with operating personnel and maintenance crews; and (5) responsibility for all regulatory compliance and monitoring reports.

An example of how the process works is offered by BioGro's contract with Appleton Papers of Roaring Springs, Pennsylvania. In its kraft paper production facility, Appleton has to dispose of liquid paper sludge. The disposal method had been to release it into a series of five-acre lagoons—until the lagoons became filled.

Land application was selected as an alternative, and BioGro was contracted for the project. Some thirty Pennsylvania farmers owning a total of about 3,500 acres in corn and hay were contacted. They liked the prospects of their soils being improved with nutrients and organic matter and agreed to participate in the program. The farms were thoroughly evaluated concerning soil type and subsurface geology. Sludge was not applied near property lines, wells, or streams. Everything was done to manage the program effectively—groundwater monitoring, soil samples, and nutrient recycling.

A report in the trade journal *Pulp and Paper* gave this description of the project:

> Local landowners have been quite pleased with the results of sludge usage. Several farmers report that fertilizer costs have been reduced $20 to $40 an acre. Other farmers have gone with a partial reduction in fertilizer rates and still obtained higher crop yields. Hay crops receiving sludge look very good, and corn receiving sludge looks as good as or better than adjacent corn not receiving sludge. In contrast to the initial resistance to the program, the company now receives as many as seven or eight requests per week for sludge application.

The increasing need to recover nutrients from wastes—to save energy rather than squander resources and to reduce tax-payer costs of skyrocketing traditional waste disposal—all are combining to make land application of such wastes as non-toxic municipal and industrial sludge a viable new industry. It is most certainly appropriate technology in action and in business.

CRAFTING FURNITURE

In an old warehouse in Saint Paul, Minnesota, Jim Roberts inspects the precise fit of the furniture he's producing—sturdy butcher block tables, slatted-seat chairs, a side table. Roberts is dwarfed by the stacks of wooden boxes, most of them labeled "California Finest Grapes." Farther beyond are bundles of small boards neatly twined, and next to the freight elevator cluster wooden crates of all kinds.

"Companies pay people to haul this wood away and dump it; I recover it and make furniture that is functional and can be knocked down if necessary." His two-and-one-half-year-old company, Crate Prospects, sells all the chairs, tables, desks, and shelves made by Roberts and his two employees at its small outlet store in Minneapolis.

Some customers are budget-conscious students; others come because they believe in what he's doing. "I think they feel they're part of a resource recovery; they're conserving," is the way Roberts explains Crate Prospects' appeal. A durable desk chair costs only $14; an Early American ladder-back chair goes for $28; a school desk is $55; and a French-style table is $150.

When he says "resource recovery," Roberts doesn't mean just wood. He's tapped the local talents of a retired machinist to help him rebuild the large-scale machines—saws, lathes, sanders—that he retrieves from the scrap piles of local industry. For only $200, he revamped an edge saw that would have cost him about $2,000 new.

The larger Twin Cities industries have come to await Jim Roberts' crate-scrounging rounds. "Now they look for me," he says. "I haul away their industrial waste for free; it's really a service, both ways." Usually he picks up the domestic crates, made of pine or poplar; he prizes the occasional Yamaha piano and motorcycle crates, constructed of Philippine hardwoods and mahogany.

Most woodworkers design furniture, then cut wood to size, but Roberts reverses the procedure. "I have to see what I've got, then draw the design." Wood used in making a chair is very close to the size it came as part of the original crate. Drawers for a small chest are the unaltered "California Finest Grapes" crates, lettered fetchingly in green—akin to such brand-name chic as the Coca Cola trays, now collectors' items. "We sell a lot of those chests," Roberts says. "Everyone's got the same shade of green carpeting in their apartment."

RENEWABLE ENERGY

As the realities of long-term energy usage surface in many ways and on many levels, small businesses active in the conservation and renewable energy field are flourishing.

In Northborough, Massachusetts, for example, G&S Mill manufactures a middle-sized waste-wood-burning furnace to provide heat to factories. Paul Kalenian, president and sole full-time employee, originally designed the furnace to meet the needs of New England sawmills that have plenty of scrap wood. His two-chamber design with a double-wall, heavily insulated firebox has an almost ninety percent combustion efficiency. One cord of wood has the energy equivalent of 200 gallons of home heating oil, and this furnace can run for roughly half the fuel cost of an oil burner.

Sunworks of Healdsburg, California, is combining collector assembly work with direct sales, installation, and services of solar systems. Owner Richard Conrat notes that small manufacturers of solar panels around the country are beginning to command a significant share of local markets. Adds Conrat:

> Based on our experience of four years, the manufacture of solar collectors is not necessarily akin to the manufacture of refrigerators and cars. Medium-temperature flat plate collectors can be economically produced in small shops around the country and sold locally. We can produce a quality collector and sell it much lower than the brand name units by *assembling* our own. Boxing and glazing collectors are labor intensive, and it makes better economic sense to assemble collectors locally than to ship fragile, bulky, preassembled collectors around the country.

Physicist Paul Ross of the University of Michigan last year called for the creation of a new profession: the "house doctor," an expert in making homes and commercial buildings more energy efficient. House doctors would obtain data developed under a wide enough range of conditions to be applicable to most home designs. According to Dr. Ross, they would be able to advise a homeowner on how much fuel costs would be saved by different strategies, such as additional insulation, a modified furnace, or new refrigerator. Dr. Ross sees house doctors as a major step toward reducing heating requirements by fifty percent. He also envisions their having a role in preventing potential health hazards from airtight homes.

Throughout the nation, a number of businesses now offer to make an energy audit on your home to find ways to eliminate areas where heat escapes in cold weather and heat penetrates in the summer.

Energy stores and companies offering energy-saving devices and services have developed around the country. In the Northeast especially, signs offering wood stoves for sale abound. The number of manufacturers of wood stoves has increased dramatically.

An old dairy barn alongside Route 30, just south of Pawlet, Vermont, is the new home of a company called Earth Services, Inc. Ron Bell is president. The structure has 7,000 square feet, with a potential for another 3,000 square feet of usable space. From the back window, the view is vintage Vermont—meandering stream in the foreground, rolling meadow beyond leading up to the Green Mountain range in the distance.

Bell had a cement floor poured where the cow stanchions had been, and two loading docks have replaced the sliding barn doors. A range of the products sold by Earth Services is stored there: wood and coal stoves, solar water heaters, chimney cleaning equipment. This variety typifies the offerings of renewable energy consumer products.

When we first visited Earth Services in 1977, the entire operation was housed in rented space across from the general store in nearby Wells. From that original space, the business has grown dramatically. Annual sales tell a large part of the story: 1977—$35,000; 1978—$150,000; 1980—$1 million.

Seventy percent of the volume is through wholesale accounts. The company has about 400 dealers, 150 of whom are really active, and 8 sales representatives covering from Minnesota to New England, and down to Virginia.

The retail store in Manchester, Vermont, which opened in mid-1980, has 3,000 square feet and offers customers everything from solar heating devices to insulating screens, with accessories ranging from fans to solar games.

Thirty-three-year-old Bell has a background in corporate finance as well as social welfare agency experience. Such combinations are not wholly unusual in the solar energy field; Peter Barnes, head of San Francisco's Solar Center, had been West Coast editor of the *New Republic* before launching his company. Bell's corporate finance background is being put to the test because of the rapid growth of Earth Services. He has to make decisions about long-term financing, handling an impressive debt load, and managing cash flow in a seasonal business.

His office area, created from a former silo, now includes a Wang microcomputer. But the difficulty of getting an even flow of electricity in rural Vermont at times creates computer confusion. And phone service in such an out-of-the-way place can present another problem. Overall, though, business building in Vermont has been relatively smooth for Earth Services' twelve employees, who now include a controller, sales director, product developer, and retail store manager.

The Earth Services' brochure carries this message:

> Earth Services, Inc. is staffed by a group of dedicated professionals with expertise in engineering, energy management, computer technology, economics, and business management. Our operating philosophy is to provide high-quality products that will reduce dependence on depletable and inflationary energy sources and provide the consumer with the free power of the sun. From the day it goes in, every Earth Services solar system says plenty about the people behind it. It has to be right.

Great Lakes Energy Systems in Boyne City, Michigan, falls into the category of an energy store. Great Lakes sells wood stoves, solar systems, and windmills. In addition, they carry solar greenhouses, furnaces and boilers, ceiling fans, insulated window shades, fireplace inserts, and many other energy-saving products, not to mention composting toilets. So far, most of Great Lakes Energy Systems' success has come from selling residential wood stoves, the bread-and-butter item that helped them ring up sales of $470,000 in 1980, their second year of operation.

Boyne City is located in a rural, sparsely populated region of Michigan. The local economy is dependent on tourists and vacation home owners, people from cities like Detroit and Chicago who come for hunting, boating, fishing, and skiing. These people, as well as the locals who cater to them, make up the base market for Great Lakes Energy Systems.

"When we started in 1979, there were ten other places that sold wood stoves within twenty miles of us," recalls Gregory "Tiny" Reinhardt, part-owner of Great Lakes. "The market here was ripe for wood stoves. To get a good start, we offered a larger selection of stoves at prices lower than our competitors. By operating at a lower profit margin we were able to outsell the competition."

Reinhardt, and his two partners Dan Ozmer and Philip Armstrong, are not newcomers to owning a business. From 1975 to 1978, Reinhardt and Armstrong had been part-owners of a stained glass business. They sold out in early 1978, bought some land, and each decided to build a home using alternative energy systems. During that same year, Ozmer had been in the wood stove business for six months, closing because his partner, a carpenter, wanted to go back to carpentry. In the fall of 1978, Reinhardt and Armstrong ran short of the cash they needed to finish construction of their homes, and in December they joined up with Ozmer to try their hands at a full-fledged energy business.

"We started the business with $14,000," says Reinhardt. "Using our personal property—the two houses—as collateral, we were able to get a $9,000 loan from the bank. The remaining $5,000 was personal capital. We set up a three-way partnership. The $14,000 was used to secure the building for the store and to buy the inventory, consisting of wood stoves, a few compost toilets, and some solar hot water tanks. Our emphasis was going to be on selling residential wood stoves."

To get going, the three did mailings to their friends and to former customers of the stained glass store. They wrote their own press releases, emphasizing that their prices were the lowest around.

"We based the business on three operating principles," says Tiny. "We provide the best selection of products, the best prices, and the best services for those products. That's our formula for success."

Previous business experience, their low pricing policy, and high-quality service have all added up to steadily growing sales at Great Lakes. Growth has been financed through additional bank loans and open accounts with their suppliers.

"Our first full year in business, 1979, was a sellers' market for wood stoves," says Tiny. "There was panic buying going on around the country. Manufacturers couldn't keep up with the business. It was a great year to start out.

"In the first year, we had $280,000 in sales, and last year, $470,000. Solar was not very good the first year, but it's picking up now. Our market is split about sixty percent wood stove-related business, twenty percent solar, and the rest divided among wind systems, compost toilets, and other accessories."

Architect Allan Hawman and his partner, Kevin Stanley, like the work they do: renovating houses, designing energy-efficient solutions for clients, and using their craftsmanship to personalize construction. Their company, Designworks, was founded in 1977.

Hawman sees his marketplace as more conventional than futuristic—more middle-class than elitist. "As the commonsense quality of solar design is better understood, our clients will increasingly see the unity between solar-oriented design and economy," predicts Hawman. So he plays down the solar features when discussing building plans with new clients, although the orientation is there and so is the final result. Designworks is headquartered in the same Victorian building in Emmaus, Pennsylvania, as *In Business.*

About 3,000 miles away, in Winters, California, is Living Systems, another solar design firm that also serves as energy conservation consultants. According to Jonathan Hammond, principal: "We specialize in passive solar buildings and self-sufficient community design as well as research and development related to these areas. We are designers, ecologists, landscape architects, mathematicians, systems analysts, artists, and craftspeople."

Living Systems has developed thermal storage techniques, inexpensive movable insulation, accurate methods of predicting thermal performance of buildings, and solar building codes for Davis, Indio, and Sacramento Counties, California. The company's recent projects include design of a passive solar-heated and solar-cooled community center in Winters, California, residential housing units using passive solar heating and cooling systems, and the design of a twenty-acre energy-efficient development at Dinuba, California, with 120 passive units.

The Solar Center in San Francisco was founded in 1976 by a few individuals who thoroughly understood, according to president Peter Barnes, that "succeeding in any small business is difficult at best. Succeeding in a small business where the market is barely emerging is more difficult still." The founding group included a former journalist and political organizer; an attorney and small businessman who had worked with Barnes in political campaigns; an architect who had coauthored a book on solar energy; a skilled carpenter who had studied alternative energy; and a young woman who had just completed a solar technician training program sponsored by the California Office of Appropriate Technology. Each of the founders purchased or pledged to purchase $5,000 worth of common stock during the first year.

"Contrary to standard business procedure," Barnes explained, "we launched the business before we had assurance that we would be able to raise the targeted amount of capital. We were anxious to get started and, being somewhat idealistic, assumed that we would find the necessary capital as we went along. In fact, we did. Within a year, several individuals loaned us a total of $39,500, and one even guaranteed a bank line of credit of $30,000. All the loans were long term and at below-market interest rates. The lenders, like us, were motivated more by a belief in solar energy than by a desire to make a high return on investment."

Barnes has continued to be innovative and aggressive in developing capital sources for the Solar Center. In 1980, he arranged with a local savings and loan association for customers to get special rates on loans via a Safe Energy Fund he helped to promote for the association.

Originally, the Solar Center envisioned itself as a kind of solar supermarket for the do-it-yourself homeowner, but that market turned out to be virtually nonexistent. "Do-it-yourselfers were either not able to afford solar equipment or so totally committed to doing things themselves that they would scrounge everything and purchase almost nothing. About eighty-five percent of our income was coming from making complete solar installations, and it soon became clear that, if we were to stay in business, we would have to become darn good full-time contractors."

Initially, most installations were solar water-heating systems in homes of friends and friends of friends. Eventually that shifted to solar water-heating systems for multiple-unit buildings. Adds Barnes, "The economics were better than average because one solar heating system could supply hot water to many units, thus lowering the per-unit cost. The economics were further helped by the newly enacted California solar tax credit, which was followed late in 1978 by a federal solar tax credit."

By mid-1980, the Solar Center had a full-time staff of ten

and full confidence that "the many seeds we've planted, and the many strengths we've worked hard to acquire, are starting to bear fruit." Besides striving to succeed as a solar business, the company also wants to succeed as an employee-owned and democratically managed business:

> Some of the ingredients of democratic management, at least as we've been practicing it, are: (1) the opportunity for all employees to become equal stock owners; (2) equal pay for all employees (with minor and temporary deviations based on need); (3) collective decision making, usually by consensus at weekly staff meetings and periodic staff retreats; and (4) clear-cut assignment of responsibilities, with accountability to the group.

Presently there are about twenty-five small manufacturers in the United States of mini-wind machines—units designed to bring a large degree of energy self-sufficiency to homes in certain areas. Estimates from the Washington, D.C.-based American Wind Energy Association indicate that the small-scale wind machine industry has about $7 million in annual sales. After studying the marketplace, writer Frank Farwell reports:

> The entrepreneurial founders and backers of these companies have realized that the most immediate source of pure energy is wind—that finicky, cooling air current that we have overlooked until now. In the short run, before more exotic, pure source energy solutions are perfected, wind may be our easiest stopgap. Today's rotors are stepchildren of the existing aerospace industry, the knowledge of which is generally available to small wind-machine designers.

The firms in the field are reaching for a special market of consumers who are ready, or nearly ready, to purchase wind machinery at prices ranging from $4,000 to $15,000, plus half again that much for tower and installation. "Within five years," predicts Kevin Morgan of Dakota Sun and Wind in Aberdeen, South Dakota, "we will be setting up an assembly line to build two or three machines per hour. We haven't done any marketing or advertising, but we know the market is there." Dakota Sun and Wind (since relocated to Denver, Colorado) expected to sell about 200 units in 1980 for revenues of about $1.5 million. Its smallest capacity model, a three-kilowatt machine, sells for $7,500 plus tower and installation.

North Wind Power Company, in Warren, Vermont, expects to sell 1,000 units annually by 1983. Most of their wind machines are designed for remote-site use, where no power lines exist. Telecommunication and navigation equipment concerns are big customers.

On the southern shore of Cape Cod, Dutch-born Herman Drees is busy keeping up with orders for his five-kilowatt, vertical-axis (Darrieus-type) "cyclo-turbine." His company, Pinson Energy Corp., will sell about one hundred of the machines this year, at $4,800 each. It all started with Drees's master's thesis at MIT, finished about the time of the first gasoline scare.

On the lower edge of Wisconsin's Kettle Morraine forest, southwest of Milwaukee, the Windworks Corp. was to have begun manufacturing ten-kilowatt machines by 1981. The windworks' thirty-three-foot rotor span makes it best suited for co-ops of homeowners, or light industrial applications. Its price tag: around $20,000.

The largest volume seller in 1980 is the Enertech Corp. of Norwich, Vermont. In a twelve-month period, company Chairman Ned Coffin reported 230 sales of their one-and-one-half-kilowatt units. Like the majority of other companies in the field, Enertech is aiming for a larger model, and now a fifteen-kilowatt machine is nearing the production stage.

Enertech employs about four dozen persons who work out of a collection of farm buildings in Norwich, and out of an ancient, wooden-planked warehouse across the Connecticut

River in Lebanon, New Hampshire. Plans for a new plant are under way.

Enertech is organized around Henry Clews, its chief engineer. Clews had been a successful windmill tinkerer in Maine during the late 1960s and attracted the attention of some editors at *National Geographic* magazine. A feature article describing Clews's progress with wind machines created a flood of interest. Enertech was formed when Coffin, then a sales agent in South Africa, organized a group of partners in the early 1970s, bought the rights to Clews's projects, and moved the new company from Maine to Norwich, across the Connecticut River from Dartmouth College.

Aero Power Systems, Inc., of Berkeley, California, has been manufacturing small wind energy conversion systems since 1971. One of its units is now furnishing electricity for the first wind-powered traffic lighting system in the United States. The purchaser was the California Department of Transportation; the location was a remote area where a rather hazardous intersection required a traffic light.

What all wind machine companies have in common is a wide streak of pioneering entrepreneurship and a limited track record: The majority of them are less than five years old. Most are currently strapped for cash and few have sales over $1 million, although in four or five years several of them could have twenty times that amount. As homeowners realize the viability of wind power, sales will be self-generating.

"If you look at the potential," comments Windworks Vice-President Rob Couchman, "there is no way there will be any real competition between manufacturers."

Established manufacturers, that is. Like most boom-now, mature-later industries in their embryonic stages, not all the starry-eyed starters will be smiling a few years into the race. Couchman adds: "In the small companies who entered the marketplace too rapidly, there will be a heavy attrition rate."

In all, there could be as many as 18 million small windmills providing direct-to-the-customer electricity by the time the market is saturated. So reports a 1979 study by the Los Alamos (California) Scientific Lab, which predicts 93 million kilowatts of installed small-scale (less than ten-kilowatt) wind machines by the mid-twenty-first century.

UNDERGROUND ARCHITECTURE

From his vantage point on Cape Cod in Brewster, Massachusetts, Malcolm Wells sees architecture developing in a new direction—underground—as more and more solar, earth-covered buildings are being designed and constructed. Wells tells his story:

> Five years ago, underground architecture was virtually unheard of in this country, but three years later it had become well enough accepted to have made the cover of *Popular Science*. Then, last year, *Newsweek* did a feature on the subject, and now I see that the *New York Times* has discovered earth-cover.
>
> I've been following all this ever since 1964, when I first got involved in underground architecture. Back in those innocent times I was able to interest people in the idea only because it seemed to them so remote. Like science fiction, it posed no immediate threat. It wasn't until years later, when I began to be taken more seriously, that the "how-will-this-affect-me" reaction set in, and people began to picture themselves living in damp basements with rats and mildew, and with all the associated terrors of darkness and burial.
>
> Fortunately, those days are pretty well behind. By now, everyone has seen or read enough about underground architecture to know that it is usually brighter, sunnier, and drier than most conventional architecture. Terraculture seems to have arrived. My practice consists of four things: designing solar, earth-covered buildings for my own clients, designing

such buildings for other architects, giving lectures on the subject, and selling books.

This new-formed popularity of underground architecture, for instance, turned my self-published information book into a booming business generator, catching my three-person office staff completely unprepared. Processing 200 book requests in a day may not sound like much, but it isn't as easy as might be imagined. Handling all that incoming mail and all those outgoing cartons, books, stamps, labels, and envelopes, not to mention all the record keeping involved, was more than we could manage. We worked in panic.

As an architect, I'd been used to dealing with maybe five or six clients a year. Payments from them required perhaps seventy-five bookkeeping entries annually. Now, we were handling that many transactions in a couple of hours! Fortunately, that first avalanche lasted only a day or two, and we had time to start organizing ourselves to handle the next one. Every favorable review in a national magazine, even a little two-line endorsement, would generate a new wave of orders. Up and down, our mail-order fortunes followed the reviews. If I learned nothing else from the whole experience, I learned to respect the power of editorial commentary.

The American underground movement is still limited pretty much to house construction. In at least forty-seven of the fifty states, a total of about 2,000 dwellings had been completed by the end of 1980. That's 2,000 unique, individual experiments, each contributing to the growing fund of underground construction experience. I'm certain that over half a million such houses will have been built by the year 2000, and an accompanying surge in the number of nonresidential buildings will have occurred as well.

Already, people who've heard of the energy and resource savings in underground houses have started to plan larger buildings. I'm already designing several—a university building in Michigan, a large housing complex in Colorado, offices, laboratories—and I know of other architects doing even bigger things. Soon there'll be no stopping this idea. Once we see that there really are ways to build less destructively, to live more cheaply, and to use fewer resources without real sacrifice, the snowball will roll. That's when a bind that's already starting to pinch will begin to hurt.

There's a shortage of people with underground know-how. I'm not just talking about architects and structural engineers and builders, although they, too, are in increasingly short supply. I'm talking about people with more peripheral kinds of know-how. There'll soon be a wide demand for the service of

- soils experts who can interpret test-boring results with an eye to construction and groundwater problems;

- waterproofing contractors able to deal knowledgeably with the scores of different systems available to meet various subgrade conditions;

- insulation contractors versed in the ways various products are damaged by soils, roots, rodents, and moisture;

- rooftop-fill contractors able to place tons of soil on carefully insulated and waterproofed roof decks without causing any damage;

- landscape architects and contractors experienced in planting rooftops and sideslopes;

- site drainage specialists;

- precast concrete technicians skilled in low-cost factory-made building parts for underground use;

- pest-control people.

Each day we get letters begging us to name someone—anyone—within, say, 500 miles of Bismarck, South Dakota, who can offer advice or help in one or more of those fields. A fledgling market is already there.

I'm not advocating the formation of brand-new companies. Not yet. Not necessarily. People already in, or qualified to be in such businesses can very easily widen their services to include the underground specialties simply by doing some after-hours reading and by experimenting on test structure or on parts of their own buildings. Once you begin to investigate any subject, you find widening circles of information that can take you as far as you care to go.

Underground construction isn't the only field that will need the new skills. Similar demands exist, or will soon exist, for people able to produce or service all the other emerging alternative technologies. There's opportunity galore for anyone resourceful enough to see it.

WOODEN BOATBUILDING

"Most people involved with crafts today are making a statement that in some way rejects a rigid, confined life style and the highly mechanized and chaotic twentieth-century world," wrote Paul Lipke in an *In Business* report on boatbuilding. Some say the revival of craft-oriented businesses, from pottery to foundry work, is the direct result of our reaction to this chaos. It is *quality* that these individuals are after and, in an important sense, appropriate technology reunites needed goods and services with the quality of the effort involved in their creation.

The skills and traditions of boatbuilding can be traced from the days of the coastal schooners through the Vikings right on back to the first hollowed-out log. Yet it is within living memory—around the turn of this century—that the craft of boatbuilding reached its zenith.

The Industrial Revolution had made possible some very innovative fastening methods, and as a result the world saw magnificent small boats turned out in large numbers. Their hull shapes beautifully adapted to local conditions through generations of slow modification, built by men with lifelong exposure to the water, the standard of excellence in these boats was extraordinary. Shortly thereafter, the internal combustion engine was adapted to marine use, and, while it freed watermen from much back-breaking work, it also precipitated a decline in the quality of boat design and associated skills. With an engine, you could move any shape through the water.

When plywood, resorcinol glues, fiberglass, and epoxy resins each made their appearance, the standards in materials changed. These innovations coincided neatly with the rapid increase in the amount of money and free time available to the American population as a whole. The result was a boom in recreational boating—and the rapid and almost total collapse of the boatbuilding and manufacturing industries as they had developed over the centuries.

The good boatbuilder was more than just a superlative woodworker; it was not unusual for him to master at least the basics of metal work, wire ropework, sailmaking, and, later, wiring, plumbing, and engine work. It is hardly surprising, then, that those builders who stayed on through the collapse and those who took up the trade later on are strong individualists. They tend to see themselves as the last survivors of a guild that had dedicated itself to tremendously high standards.

Walter Baron started in house carpentry and later worked in a local repair yard; he has spent his entire life in close contact with the sea in his town of Wellfleet, Massachusetts, on Cape Cod. His investment in the Old Wharf Dory Company began at home with an investment of a few hundred dollars in materials and a box of hand tools. Five years, a tax consultant, a production line of eight-foot prams, and some shrewd decisions later, the Old Wharf Dory Company is in the black and has just completed a new shop of 1,200 square feet.

Baron's early investments were more or less haphazard, as is usually the case in craft-oriented businesses. As it became clear that there was a demand for his skills, he put more and more effort into the business side of the shop. Five years ago he was not planning his inventory as carefully, writing off his shop and vehicle expenses, or printing brochures, but now he is. He sells hard-to-find marine fasteners and supplies at twenty percent off list price—a sideline that is netting him about fifteen percent of his gross. He also watches the shop's cash flow carefully. "The trick is to plot its course, redirect it now and then, and just take off little bits as it goes by."

Walter has taken a custom craft with a history as romantic, creative, and challenging as any other, one with a high per-unit materials/labor cost, and by being flexible in the kinds of work he does and rigid in his adherence to an expanded concept of quality has found a way to make that craft pay. In the end, he'll be in a much better position to build all-varnish yachts (if he wants to) than his equally skilled but starry-eyed competitors.

THE HUNDRED-MILES-PER-GALLON VEHICLE

Thirty-seven-year-old Dave Edmonson incorporated H-M-Vehicles in August 1977, to produce and market the Free-Way vehicle he had invented seven years earlier. Dave has a mechanical engineering degree from the University of Minnesota, was employed in the Graphic Systems of 3M Company, and later became a project manager for the Toro Company.

The "Free-Way Electric" was first shown at the 1978 EV Expo in Philadelphia. Since then it has been developed from the prototype to a limited production schedule, with over 1,000 orders as of mid-1980 and more than forty on the road. Writes Edmonson: "Our goal is to have a vehicle capable of limited freeway use (fifty-five mph) and a forty-mile range. Our current models are capable of forty-five mph and a round trip of twenty miles."

Edmonson maintains that his one-person three-wheeled commuter vehicle is the modern equivalent of a horse and will solve the high-fuel, high-maintenance problems that plague car owners. The Free-Way Electric weighs about 700 pounds and is 115 inches long, 53 inches wide, and 51 inches high.

Price in 1980 was under $3,000, varying with type of engine and other options. It's available with either gasoline, diesel, or electric power. "The 340-cc engine provides enough power, and we guarantee one-hundred miles per gallon in all types of driving," says Edmonson. All models have fiberglass bodies with a 360-degree protective steel frame. According to *AutoWeek,* the hydraulic disc brakes complement the three-wheeled design, midengine location, and standard instrumentation panel. The cast-iron engine features solid-state ignition, tapered roller bearings, a twenty-amp flywheel-driven alternator, and electric start.

Edmonson's firm employs twelve persons, who turn out sixty cars each month. Production is on the increase, as firms in Florida and California have been granted manufacturing licenses. "Progress has been a bit slower than I had hoped," comments Edmonson, "but the enthusiasm of the public really keeps us going."

6

Traditional Business with a Twist

When we originally began digging into the under-
pinnings of America's new business movement, we sought out
the nontraditional—the alternatives to the *Fortune 500*, to the
brand-name stores in suburban malls, to the fast-food franchises. Our search led us initially to the kinds of enterprises
described in the previous chapter on appropriate technology
businesses. But the more we searched, the more we realized
the significant part "traditional" businesses were playing in
this new business dream. The qualities we looked for could be
found in the old-fashioned mom-and-pop-type family restaurant, cheese shop, watch repair place, corner grocery store,
small inn, brewery, garage, small farm—and on and on. There
was really little, if anything, nontraditional about the types of
products or the services being performed. Nor were the individuals we met—the men and women who were running the
businesses—singularly nontraditional. In fact, we began to
realize that tradition is on the side of the new entrepreneurs.
If anyone lacks "roots," it is the business people who are prob-

ably in the majority today, those working for big corporations and government agencies.

In this chapter, we'd like to focus on the different twists being given to traditional businesses. Certain important themes are basic to the reasons the businesses were begun, how they are managed, and the directions they are taking. Personal life styles and personal goals usually surface very quickly in an interview with small business owners. They don't perceive themselves as hard-nosed would-be millionaires or as chief executive officers sipping J&B Scotch or leaning against a Mercedes. Given their own financial dollar, their personal and physical investment, there's no question that profits are important, but the total environment doesn't reflect single-minded bottom-line maximization. Once they turn the corner from start-up survival to market penetration, growth *management* becomes more critical than growth *opportunity*. And quality always remains a key issue. Following are some businesses that illustrate these operating principles.

LOCAL TASTES IN BEER

The Miller Brewing Company and its major competitor, Anhauser-Busch, live with intense competitive rivalry. The executives at the Straub Brewery—most of them related to the founder—live far differently.

These breweries are all successful. Miller nets profits in the millions and produces at maximum capacity, and consumers nationwide are making it "Miller time." Straub is also producing at maximum capacity, but here is where the story changes. Their maximum capacity is not determined by the potential number of consumers they might serve. At the Straub Brewery, maximum capacity is directly related to the owners' life styles.

"We only make so much and that's it. All the Straubs like

to hunt and fish too much. Besides, we're selling all we make now," says Gibby Straub.

Started by Gibby's grandfather in 1872, the Straub Brewery is located in Saint Marys, Pennsylvania, an industrial town of 7,500. Five years ago, the Straubs felt more pressure than usual from national competitors in their local market. Although they still had their loyal locals, they felt that their beer was too similar to other pilsners selling for the same price. Gibby and Herb Straub, the brewmasters, decided that one way to compete without going into a major advertising campaign would be to produce a beer that was nothing like any the competitors offered. After doing market research, the Straubs learned that one kind of beer not being brewed was an all-natural, all-grain beer—no sugar, syrups, salt, or preservatives.

The local nature of their market made the production of an all-natural beer feasible. Preservatives could be eliminated because the Straubs supply distributors with smaller amounts of beer and restock more frequently. Also, the local nature of the market allowed the Straubs to stay on top of their customers' reactions to the new-tasting beer.

"We could never operate this brewery in a city or suburban area," comments Herb Straub. "Our biggest advantages are being close to our market and knowing many of our customers on a first-name basis. We really can control our market, thus controlling our production, leaving us the option to create as much free time as we would like for hunting and fishing."

If you told Gibby or Herb Straub that they were part of the new American business movement, they would probably think you were crazy. For the Straubs, their business makes sense: It yields them a nice profit, they know many of their customers, it doesn't wear them down to the bone, and it fits into their life style. For them, profit maximization and market exploitation would mean disrupting that life style. They don't have an advertising budget or a desire to open a chain of amusement parks. Their traditional business with a twist has allowed them to survive. Tapping into the local market and mixing business with life style is the twist.

QUALITY AND GROWTH

Carolyn Golembesky has been in business for two years. Owner of Limeydowns Ltd., a custom-made down quilt business, Golembesky has some very definite feelings about growth, feelings that add a twist to her "traditional" craft business.

"I work on the slow growth philosophy," explains Golembsky. "I suppose business experts would call it managing growth!"

I began making down quilts as a hobby. Several years ago, friends wanted to buy some, and bingo, I found myself in business. My prices are fairly competitive with the store-bought quilts, but my quality is much better. Even with such a marketable product, I don't feel that my business skills are adequate for growing fast. Some people come up with a very marketable product and grow so fast that they create a monster without the skills to manage it.

Right now, I'm working on diversifying my product line and streamlining my production. Our next big step is to decide whether we want to participate in the trade shows—the big leagues. Right now, if we took a booth and got 400 orders, we'd be exceeding our capacity, lowering our quality and our good two- to three-week turnaround time. Applying the slow growth theory to the trade shows, this year we'll just attend one, see if it's worth our while, and then the following year we may take a booth. This sounds pretty obvious, but it's the sort of growth that I can manage.

My philosophy of financing lends itself to slow growth. I refuse to take out any loans, so I need to grow to have the cash reserves in order to buy the machinery to expand.

The Party Box was founded in 1967, in Jane Wilson's New York City apartment. Expertise in specialty and quantity cooking along with positive reactions from friends trying new recipes gave her the confidence needed to turn cooking experimentation into a business. Using only a $200 freezer in her bedroom and a tiny kitchen, Wilson prepared party boxes and custom catering services for entertaining. She operated out of her apartment for the first year and a half.

"When do you take a business out of your home? In my case," explains Wilson, "what tipped the cart was an order from *Sports Illustrated* for a 450-person cocktail party for the Mexican Olympic team reception. While various friends throughout New York stirred gallons of seviche, fried conch fritters, and whipped up guacamole, I realized that extra help alone was not the answer. More space and larger equipment were paramount. And a much larger investment in my business."

Maintaining the quality of their food was not a problem in the transition to cooking for larger numbers. "You can cook perfectly for 1,000 people without resorting to frozen foods. This drive for quality is rough, but the result is that everybody recognizes the effort; it's something women are known for. As a matter of fact, with many small businesses, quality may be the only reputation you have."

Life for the Party Box has not been all rosy. It has been plagued with cash flow problems, and growth has been bumpy.

The key to this business is staying as small as you can, as long as you can. I was told that a small business start-up faces bankruptcy at least three times. I wish I had heard that from the beginning; it would have made our growth and ebb and flow less frightening. The first crisis in my case was no working capital and no management experience.

In the second crisis, we almost expanded into bankruptcy. Since our kitchen was so small we decided to try and find more room in our landlord's building and in other locations. A store came open around the corner in our building. First, we were going to redo that into a kitchen, but costs made it easier to retile and bring the existing kitchen up to better standards and use the new space for an office and storage. The contractor gave us an estimate of $10,000 to redo the kitchen. It cost $20,000 and it was done in the summer at a low point in business. Personal loans made it possible for us to survive that time as banks still did not want to give us working capital. About as far as they like to go for a small business is new equipment.

Some of the pitfalls that can put you over the precipice and that happened to us are over inventory; too many people in help for the amount of business, which takes too much money out of the business; too much income taken out by the owners; and not reseeding the business by buying new equipment to meet growth needs.

Handling growth has been Wilson's biggest challenge in her version of a traditional food service business. For Wilson, quality is her business, her bread and butter. She will never substitute corn syrup and artificially flavored cocoa for real chocolate. Instead, she would sooner eliminate the item completely, substituting a different high-quality dessert. The price of her service is usually three and a half times the cost of the food. Thus her customers are paying for the quality. But then again, their best source of new customers is referrals. It's a circle that leads to profits and lots of personal satisfaction.

NEW TRICKS IN THE BOOK TRADE

Who would want to distribute books to a 3,000-square-mile region containing the largest wilderness in the continental United States? The North Country Book Express, owned and operated by Ivar Nelson and Patrica Hart. With $5,000 and the zeal of Lewis and Clark, they began a process that over the past few years has transformed itself into several coevolving

operations, each tuned to the particular economic requirements of the northern Rockies.

Their twist was placing production closer to consumption—regional creation and distribution of information.

Wholesaling is a nickel-and-dime operation, Terry Lawhead explained in a report on North Country Book Express.
A potential inventory necessarily depends upon the function
of value and weight leading to profit. In the case of North
Country, books occupy little space but have high value per
pound. There was reason to believe the scale could work.

North Country Book Express steadily lost money. Book-
sellers did indeed buy gratefully beyond expectation—$20,000
worth in the second month with virtually no returns. But certain logistical problems appeared insurmountable. Vast dis-
tances made it difficult to keep the van stocked as titles sold
out toward the end of the route. The popularity of the select
inventory, held to less than one hundred titles due to lack of
space, attested to the demand for information covering wild-
life and plant identification, history and novels set in the area,
cookbooks, and texts on self-reliance. But expenses were
devouring commissions on sales; the system was a failing
success.

Nelson and Hart knew from the start that that would be so.
Their losses were an investment, equivalent to the cost of a
post-graduate degree in a communications field. "We had
decided to learn the ass end first," Nelson says. "While working as a farrier several years ago, I knew the business end of
the horse was its feet, not the head, although the head certainly became useful somewhat later." Nelson and Hart kept
their jobs at the library and bookstore, took loans and a deep
breath, and moved into their next planned phase: publishing
their own books.

"Ivar and I started the distribution network with a single
small publisher in mind—ourselves," says Hart. "We had
invested in our own typesetting equipment and took in job
work to cover expenses. Most printers do not have the facili-

ties, time, or desire to design a book for a potential printing customer, and we began producing local histories."

North Country Book Express always had a plan, a method to the apparent madness of losing money, concludes Lawhead in his account of the company. A structure that could endure had to be built. "We knew that pricing, packaging, and, most of all, distribution were the weak links for the small publisher," says Hart:

> We set out to establish an effective regional distribution system first. There is no doubt that setting up that and a production system for our books contributed greatly to their success, although the distribution and production systems themselves are not highly profitable enterprises. As we put more of our own titles into the systems, however, we find that the distribution and studio are now paying for themselves, because overhead is reduced, systems continue to work at increased capacity, and percentage of profit on each book sold is increased.

North Country Book Express worked in reverse in market development. They saw products that had potential but recognized the lack of a delivery system. By starting with the distribution end first, while maintaining other work, not taking a complete plunge, they tested the waters before jumping in and then added the diving board.

AUTOMOBILE REPAIR

"What does Curtis Circus know that Detroit doesn't?" Carter Henderson asked in the introduction of an *In Business* piece about Scott Curtis, who fixes up old Citroen automobiles in Santa Clara, California. At thirty-nine, Curtis calls himself the "head clown" at a garage called Curtis Circus. His auto repair and restoration business is flourishing while the once mighty U.S. auto industry fights for its life.

Curtis, according to Henderson, is meeting new demands which will intensify as American consumers struggle to cope with the economic mess. His methods include:

- meeting consumer demands for longer-lasting products

- cutting product costs by using "remanufactured" old parts with years of useful life left in them

- saving customers money by involving them in product maintenance

- building a reputation for excellence, which these days can enable even the smallest business to create a demand for its work among customers virtually anywhere in the world.

The Curtis Circus was started in 1969 and has grown into a $200,000-a-year business with Scott as the sole full-time employee (but with help from his wife, three children ages ten to fifteen, and two part-time mechanics). Curtis restores old Citroens so skillfully that thirteen of his customers already have put more than one million miles on their cars. He maintains a "core bank" of Citroen front-brake assemblies and other parts—produced whenever he gets free time—that can be instantly installed or shipped to a distant customer as needed. "We try desperately to remanufacture as many parts as possible using present-day technology," Scott says. As a result, many of these assemblies contain restored parts Scott has been collecting for years. Scott has developed and builds twenty-seven different easy-to-install kits, priced from $20 to $89.50, to simplify the maintenance and improve the performance of old Citroens.

Since he first started working on Citroens, Scott has urged his customers to help him maintain their cars, and he has prepared illustrated step-by-step instruction sheets to help them do it. "By teaching customers how to look after their own vehicles, beginning with simple things like cleaning, waxing, changing the oil, keeping tire pressure up, and so on, you get them more enthusiastic about their cars," he says. "Pretty soon they're calling in and saying 'Hey Scott, it's been 40,000 miles since I changed my air filter. What should I do?' So I sell them the parts, and they supply the labor for this simple job. If I had to do it myself I'd lose my butt, since I couldn't justify charging my thirty-six dollar hourly rate."

Scott started out with $1,000 in cash and an inventory of new Citroen parts worth about $500. In addition, he had quite an array of used parts cannibalized from thirteen or fourteen cars he had been given to tear apart, plus a half-dozen trailerloads of used parts.

Scott launched the Curtis Circus with a base of 150 satisfied customers. He's since expanded that to more than 1,500 with a little advertising in Citroen-owner publications and a lot of word-of-mouth advertising, which has brought him in as much business as he can handle.

YE OLDE COUNTRY INN

In May 1976, Tom and Betsey Guido signed the papers making them the owners of the Chester Inn in Chester, Vermont. After five years, the Guidos agree that their thirty-one-room inn has more than met their original criteria of a rural business that would allow them to work together and that would be fun and profitable. They related these experiences to Kris Hundley.

"We both draw salaries, but they're not very big," says Tom Guido. "If you're a good innkeeper, you figure you'll get your money out in the long run. In the meantime, you're getting other benefits that make up for the dollars." Adds Betsey Guido, "You may not make lots of money, but it's a better way of life." Confirms Jim Howard, who handles about a dozen inn sales annually through his Country Business Services: "Inn owners with only a few thousand dollars of taxable income can lead a life style comparable to a city couple with $50,000 to $70,000 of income."

Tom and Betsey Guido really run three businesses in one within their sprawling Victorian structure situated four and one-half hours north of New York City. There's a gourmet restaurant on the inn's first floor, which is open to the public six nights each week and serves an average of ninety dinners on a Saturday night. Van Gogh's, a recently renovated bar and lounge area offers drinks and weekday lunches in another corner of the spacious building. Upstairs, there are the thirty-one rooms, which can accommodate up to seventy guests. With room rates averaging twenty-three dollars per person per night (double occupancy), Guido has learned that it's much easier to make money in the rooms and the bar than in the restaurant. "The restaurant is the draw and always will be, but the rooms are the key."

It's not unusual that a country inn should combine these three businesses. As Howard puts it, "Your guests are going to have three immediate needs to be satisfied. They'll be hungry, thirsty, and tired." But Howard always reminds potential innkeepers to scale the size of their business to their goals. "If you're retired and don't need the support but just want to cover your living expenses, a small place with maybe five guest rooms and a forty-seat restaurant is enough. But if you're ambitious you'll want a sizable estate with maybe twenty rooms and up."

The Guidos bought their inn (which includes four acres, a swimming pool, and tennis courts) in 1976 for $350,000. Looking back on his down payment of about twenty-five percent, Guido believes he was seriously undercapitalized. "One mistake I made was that I should have gotten more money when I went to the local bank. You should get as much as you can and more."

Jim Howard suggests that down payments should range from twenty-five to forty percent of the purchase price and that owners should have working capital of between $10,000 and $25,000, "depending on the time of the year you'll be opening." As far as assessing the market value of country inns today, Howard says a rule-of-thumb is that an inn will sell for about $20,000 per guest room. "This formula applies to good quality inns with good locations and no deferred maintenance. This sort of place will typically be doing a minimum of $6,000 per year per room in room income, equivalent or double that figure in food income, and fifty percent of that figure in bar income."

COMMUNITY ECONOMIC DEVELOPMENT

What do you get when several women in a rural community want to have a say in their economic future? In Big Stone Gap, Virginia, population 5,000, you get the cooperatively owned and managed Bread and Chicken House.

Judith Gaines, editor of the *News Journal of Rural American Women,* described several examples of women-owned country businesses that unite people and local resources.

It all began in 1971 when Catherine Rumschlag, Illinoise Mitchell, and three others decided that, instead of trying to plug into the existing economic system, which never met their needs very well, they could create their own alternative. "We asked ourselves, what do we do best? The answer was: bake bread and cakes and fry chicken. It seemed kind of strange to have a business that did just that, but when a building and some equipment became available, we said, 'Why not?'"

Ten years later, the Bread and Chicken House is a community institution, providing morning donuts to local miners, lunch for kids in the summer recreation program, and baked goods to schools and churches and community group functions. Clubs can hold meetings in the party room adjoining the bakery. Senior citizens get a ten percent discount on anything in the place. And no one who comes there is turned away hungry.

Plenty of people, however, do pay. The business grossed $260,000 last year, which, as Catherine Rumschlag puts it, "is an awful lot of German chocolate cake," one of the bakery's specialties.

Another rural enterprise described by Judith Gaines is Coal Lamp Originals in Williamsburg, Kentucky, started by Marian Colette two years ago.

Williamsburg is an area where "coal and dole" have been the mainstays of the economy; where big government, big business, and foreign corporations have controlled development from afar; where plain old poverty and the lack of such basic amenities as safe drinking water have discouraged business people from living in the community. For women, the problems are particularly severe. That's why a business like Coal Lamp Originals takes on so much significance. Writes Gaines:

> Coal Lamp Originals began with resources nobody else was using: lamp shades and parts from rummage sales or which somebody donated; chunks of coal too low in heat-producing power to be commercially marketable; a moldy, empty basement; women who had no training in making lamps or running a business but who needed jobs. They formed a co-op so that all the workers would share profits in proportion to their labor. Their product: a piece of Appalachia, a lamp marketed to draw on the tourists' attraction to mountain culture and on the sentimental attachment local folks have to the curse and the blessing of the region: coal.

Adds Marian Colette: "If the women worked at a big factory, they might produce more, but they wouldn't advance themselves any. I've heard lots of women say, 'I'd rather take less wages and work some place where I have something to say about what goes on.'"

Coal Lamp Originals is one of several businesses started and supported by the Mountain Women's Exchange, a coalition of seven nonprofit organizations in southeastern Kentucky and northern Tennessee. All seven organizations, composed primarily of women, believe that rural mountain women need to assert their voices in their communities and to increase their economic options.

From all over the country, we are finding examples of how small businesses are sparking an economic revitalization of both urban and rural areas. Only a few years ago, urban renewal was begun with a bulldozer. Today it is being done by the opening of new small businesses. Abandoned main streets in cities and towns are coming back thanks to the many conventional businesses whose twist is their obvious benefit to their communities—the locale from which they operated.

Stewart Perry, president of the Institute for New Enterprise Development in Cambridge, Massachusetts, has been closely observing America's new small business movement during its rapid growth of the past ten to fifteen years.

In the January-February 1981 issue of *In Business*, Perry wrote a guest editorial to answer the question: Where did this new small business movement come from? His answer dwells at length upon community economic development and provides additional insights into why a twist has been added to the conventional business environment.

Paradoxically, perhaps the earliest source (of vitality for this movement) was the ferment of the 1960s, the counterculture, the antiestablishment movements that attacked business and its values, along with the other established institutions of the society. Thus, by 1974, according to a Harris poll commissioned by a Senate committee, Americans as a group distrusted business and most of the other major institutions of our society. By 1975, only eighteen percent of the public had any confidence in business. But something else was building up, unrecognized, during that same period.

Members of the counterculture, hippies and others who had sought independence from the American middle-class values and practices they detested so much and who were also turned off by ordinary establishment careers were leading the way into the new business movement. At first, counterculture people had opened art shops, boutiques, and head shops to serve their own group in the special neighborhoods like Haight-Ashbury, but they soon moved into restaurants, clothing, furniture, and even housing—if you count minor repairs, renovations, housepainting, and the like. The counterculture people had discovered that they could be independent and self-respecting and have fun by providing basic goods and services, at first to people in their own community but later to an expanding market. They found themselves—horrors!—in business. Of course, a lot of other not-so-hippie souls also discovered that there were new counterculture markets out there to be explored. But the hippies had served as a model for others who were not content with the old ways, others who came to carve their own niches in a wider range of ventures, building upon their own different interests, experiences, and training. Without quite knowing it, out of the turmoil of the late 1960s and early 1970s America began recapturing something important from its old traditions of self-reliance and of building a stake in society by one's own efforts. The countercultural movement had paradoxically succeeded in imbuing a new energy for the entrepreneurial traditions of our society.

But the rediscovery of entrepreneurship in America was not just the province of the young middle-class women and men who had the resources and motivation to go into business for themselves. Nor was it merely an individualistic matter, part of the "me generation" thrust toward self-expression. First, members of the less advantaged groups of our society have also participated in the increased interest in business development. And, second, there has also been a kind of collectivist dimension within the new business movement. That is, groups as well as individuals have sought to make their way via business—in cooperatives, communes, and other worker-owned enterprises. This sector of activity, interestingly enough, has even generated support for legislative initiatives: the National Consumer Cooperative Bank (which also serves production co-ops); changes in the SBA authorization to encourage support of worker-owned ventures; and a variety of community-based economic development programs.

In fact, business development programs as part of community-based economic development have been an especially significant sector of the new attitude toward business; and here neither individualist nor middle-class values are necessarily involved. Community-based programs have especially arisen in poor minority neighborhoods.

Often in those neighborhoods business development is viewed as the critical element in revitalizing the neighborhood; so, on occasion, local residents of all levels and occupations have banded together to provide additional incentives for others in the neighborhood to go into business. What might be called social entrepreneurship and even social venture capital has appeared in such neighborhoods and in some rural areas, in innovative economic institutions. These institutions, usually called community development corporations (CDCs), foster local business by programs of assistance and investment. The CDCs usually had their roots in the civil rights movement and the antipoverty programs of the 1960s. Today these new institutions—governed by broad coalitions of community residents—hold great promise for business development just where new businesses are most needed: in the deteriorated inner cities of metropolitan areas and in underdeveloped rural districts. The basic political foundations of the CDCs were expressed in a philosophy of economic empowerment: If the local community can sponsor, promote, or sometimes even own a significant part of the productive elements of the local economy, the people of that community will move into the mainstream of society instead of marking time on its margins.

7

Building a Business: Principles for Managing Your Finances

No matter what business you start, friends invariably ask probing questions. Why are you doing what you're doing? Do you know what you're doing? Where will you get the money, and do you have enough? And, of course, they wonder—but perhaps do not ask—Have you lost your marbles?

This chapter gives some of the approaches and principles that are fundamental to developing a solid small business but that are too often ignored. I don't know anyone who follows each to the letter; in our own case, for example, I have to admit when pressed that we have not yet completed a comprehensive (or for that matter, incomprehensive) business plan.

The following information is offered by some of the most capable people we've come across in the small-business field. As each of us forges ahead in the early days of our venture, it makes sense to learn well the wisdom that has helped others before us to succeed.

FINANCING A NEW BUSINESS

Coming up with the money for getting started is the first problem a would-be entrepreneur faces. Of the many possible ways of capitalizing a business, those entrepreneurs who make up the new small-business movement tend to find ways that allow them to manage the business as they choose.

Friendly Money

In a survey of *In Business* readers, we found that sixty percent financed their businesses through funds supplied by themselves, friends, or relatives. Thus three out of five persons began their enterprises with "friendly money." Of the balance, almost thirty percent went for conventional bank loans, eight percent issued stock, and two percent used venture capital.

In our judgment, that sixty percent figure is an accurate reflection of the funding route taken by today's new entrepreneurs. Friendly money—sometimes classified as informal risk capital—is a key to the development of the kinds of personalized, quality-oriented businesses springing up in the 1980s. In a listing of twelve sources of small-business financing, Fred Beste of the Kentucky Highlands Investment Corporation places "yourself" as number one:

> If you've got the money, there is no easier source to convince than yourself that you are a great investment risk. Most institutional investors will require a substantial personal investment (relative to your net worth) prior to their investment, anyhow. And you need not have it in the form of cash on hand; with the recent nationwide run-up in real estate values, for example, many entrepreneurs are finding $20,000–$40,000 or more available to them by taking out a second mortgage on their house.

William Wetzel of the University of New Hampshire's Whittemore School of Business sees the availability of friendly money as "a key to our economic strategy for revitalizing New England small business." Under his direction, the university's Center for Industrial and Institutional Development launched a research effort to determine the cost and availability of informal risk capital for firms without access to traditional venture capital sources or the public equity markets. The research is designed to improve the availability of risk capital for inventors, entrepreneurs, and dynamic small firms and to increase the opportunities available to risk capital investors. Informal risk capital investors tend to be financially sophisticated individuals of means, often having previous investment or management experience with entrepreneurial ventures.

Wetzel cites Robert McCray of Manchester, New Hampshire, as an example of friendly money in action. McCray had been manager and later chief stockholder of a company called Worcester Controls Corporation. He had started there in the early 1950s and proceeded to build the annual sales of the business from $500,000 to more than $40 million. The company was on the American Stock Exchange when he sold out in 1978.

Since then, McCray has been actively involved in helping young people who are anxious to form their own companies. One of the companies he's associated with now is organized by two people he used to work with at Worcester Controls. His relationship with another company, Business Helicopters, came about when the founder tried to sell him a helicopter.

McCray sees his present activities—helping to finance young companies, offering his services as a kind of senior consultant and then selling back his equity in the company when it becomes profitable—as a way of providing the same kind of opportunities he was given by the original owner of Worcester Controls. McCray is an extraordinary case of how beneficial the combination of friendly money and friendly advice can be to start-up companies.

Pooled Funds

Although not exactly classifiable as informal risk capital, the concept of using pooled funds in a way that benefits the public is being undertaken by a San Francisco Savings and Loan Association. The creative financing plan was developed by Peter Barnes and his colleagues at the Solar Center, in conjunction with Jerome Dodson, president of San Francisco's Continental Savings. At the urging of the Solar Center and others, depositors are encouraged to specify their deposits (including standard money market certificates) as for investment in something called the Safe Energy Fund. The money is used to provide long-term financing for people who want to install or convert to solar heating systems (see also pages 99–101).

The financing differs from most property improvement loans, and it benefits both the borrower and businesses. The interest rate to borrowers is one and one-half percent above the average interest rate paid to Safe Energy Fund depositors, which puts it below the rate charged by most banks to their prime corporate customers. The plan allows the borrower to spread the initial conversion cost over the lifetime of the system, so a long-term pay-back of up to twenty years is possible, with monthly payments immediately less than the cost of conventional energy. It benefits business like the Solar Center because customers can go ahead and purchase solar design services and units.

Deferred Gratification

Deferred gratification is the term used by Ed Flaherty, president of Rapid Oil Change in Eden Prairie, Minnesota, to describe the need for new enterprises to finance themselves through retained earnings. The Minneapolis entrepreneur has started five new companies in the past ten years. Each start-up has followed a careful outline of criteria to build an enterprise with very little equity capital.

Flaherty's principle is to select a venture that does not

require heavy initial capital. When he is in the critical stage of start-up, he has another source of income available to cover his living expenses for the first twelve months. This way, if projections fail to materialize, he is not caught in a position where he and the business are both depleting its valuable resource—money. Says Flaherty:

> The start of any new venture places a lot of stress upon a person. The last thing that an entrepreneur needs is the family and personal pressure placed upon him by the lack of money. I've personally always lived conservatively. This keeps my family overhead low and allows me to start ventures that don't require me to draw $2,000 per month or more to live. As I've made money, I've then paid cash for personal increases in living standards to keep that overhead low. Any aspiring entrepreneur must realize that business and personal financial lives are one-hundred percent connected. Both have to have spartan and efficient operations to succeed.

The thirty-four-year-old Flaherty's "ten-minute oil change business" was started four years ago with $1,000 invested capital and an $8,400 bank loan. He now has a chain of seventeen locations, annual sales of more than $3 million, pretax earnings exceeding $100,000, and assets approaching $1 million.

About financing, Flaherty points out that the business was perfectly set up to grow from internal cash flow because he was not continually tying up a high portion of the company's earnings in accounts receivable or inventory.

MANAGING GROWTH

Professors Arnold Cooper of Purdue and Karl Vesper of the University of Washington have worked on models that attempt to classify stages of a venture's development from the earliest hope of the entrepreneur through later growth. In his latest study, Dr. Cooper defines four stages: *pre-start-up, start-*

up, early growth, and *later growth.* These, of course, are not necessarily a part of all businesses' growth schemes; the process could stop or stabilize at any stage.

At pre-start-up, the entrepreneur begins to develop an idea for his business. To varying extents, he may make deliberate plans by arranging contacts, checking resources, and searching out specific entrepreneurial opportunities. The process may seem quite methodical and organized or entirely unplanned, an almost predestined sequence of events. Nevertheless, at this level initial decisions are made based on the psychological and sociological background of the entrepreneur and on the environment in which he plans to locate his business.

At the start-up stage, decisions are made to establish the business at a particular time and place. Again, the entrepreneur may systematically analyze all risks and awards involved in the new venture, or he may simply dive in, seemingly blind to the problems he might face. At any rate, the business is off and running, already more successful than the innumerable dreams that never come out into the open. Writes Cooper,* "For every business that is started, how many are conceived, analyzed to some degree, and then dropped? Or how many are put on 'hold' as a dream that might someday be realized? I know of no studies of new business 'stillbirths' but suspect that, for every new firm started, there are many that never get beyond the idea or dream stage."

For businesses that are started, a third stage, that of early growth, sets in. The original idea is tested as feedback comes in from the marketplace. At this stage, the organization is small enough for the founder/owner to have a hand in all decisions at practically all levels, from ordering paper to seeking capital. According to Cooper:

*Arnold Cooper, "Entrepreneurship–Small Business Interface." Proceedings, Conference on Research and Education in Entrepreneurship, Baylor University, 1980.

As the organization develops its organization chart may look somewhat like a wheel, with the founder at the hub of reporting relationships. Control is typically maintained through direct contact with operations, rather than through formal processes. Although these control methods may appear to lack sophistication, they can give the founder a "feel" for the realities of the marketplace and for operational problems that can hardly be duplicated through formal reporting systems. These attributes make it possible for the small firm to be extremely flexible, to change not only operations but also strategy if the founder becomes convinced these changes are necessary. Of course, even though there is potential flexibility, many small firms do not change much, either because of lack of environmental pressures to do so or an inability or unwillingness of the owner to change.

At this stage, most small companies stabilize and grow very little. Seventy-nine percent of all businesses have fewer than five employees and, as such, depend greatly upon the strength of the founder for their success. Often, when the owner of such a firm grows old or dies, the company dies too unless a second generation takes over.

Companies that continue to grow enter the later growth stage in which a management team is built and the founder/ owner is less and less involved in the nitty-gritty aspects of the business. Formality develops and policies and procedures begin to take shape. Some firms develop into what Cooper calls "stable, high profit businesses," which often begin to run themselves, with the owner playing a back-seat role from the golf course or country club.

Other firms might be called "high growth potential businesses," with greater potential for continued growth and expansion. In time, these companies can become quite large and productive if the growth is managed sensibly and the founder learns to delegate various responsibilities and to control through organized, formal methods. It is important that external funds be supplied without considerable loss of control and that management be extremely strong. Risks must be taken to broaden product lines, add facilities, and build the organization. Much hard work is needed for success.

Recent research by Alan Filley and Ramon Aldag, authors of *The Regional Environment for Small Business and Entrepreneurship* (Milwaukee: Center for Venture Management, 1979), suggests that the use of formal management methods and the objectives of the firm could be related to the kinds of people who start a particular firm. Thus, *craft* entrepreneurs seem to enjoy handling production problems, wish to avoid risk, and, therefore, try to make a comfortable living without taking too many chances. Management methods are usually informal and change rate is low. *Promotion* entrepreneurs, on the other hand, are often directed toward short-term opportunities and use fluid policies centrally controlled by a chief executive. *Administrative* entrepreneurs are interested in building formal organizations with clear hierarchical systems. According to Filley and Aldag, the institution of these formal methods permits future growth. Other studies have supported these findings and suggest that different motivations and personal goals are reflected in different growth rates for various firms.

However, many entrepreneurs give little thought to their personal business goals and may not even realize that they can manage and even limit growth. Eventually they may find their company either not growing at all or, even worse, growing too much and too fast.

Joseph M. Frye, Jr., vice-president of Kentucky Highlands Investment Corporation, advises every businessperson to

be deciding now what your business philosophy is—slow growth and stability or more rapid growth, coupled with changing demands on you personally and on your abilities. The "downside" to not doing this now may be a hasty and perhaps regrettable decision made under pressure later on. I have met too many entrepreneurs who are unhappy running a large company yet who could have chosen to stay small and stable if only they had thought about it before that large order came in.

In order to plan your business future, Frye urges developing a "management succession plan" that details the company's future needs for employees and skills. It will help you keep your goals (say, ten years down the line) in mind and keep you from finding yourself run by a company snowballing out of your control.

The large company makes different demands on its owner and often requires different management skills than a smaller business. In addition, Frye points out:

> The larger company makes different demands on you as a person. Just as parents often find it difficult to allow a child to act and think on its own without the constant parental supervision, so you may find it difficult to stop working those fourteen- to eighteen-hour days. The total immersion in the business that you found necessary in starting it up may be a detriment when it becomes a more mature company. The new venture requires creativity and innovation, whereas the stable venture requires management and maybe even routine. You must be able to recognize these new demands and accommodate them, if you and your venture are to survive success.

PLUMBING YOUR CASH FLOW*

Understanding cash flow is no more difficult than understanding the plumbing that makes water usable and useful in your home. When you understand the cash flow plumbing in your business, you will be better able to make your money energy flow more smoothly to avoid wasteful spills, leaks, and shortages.

Figure 1 depicts a business as consisting of three reservoirs connected by pipes. Business operations cause money energy

*Based on a report by Don Stone in *In Business*. All illustrations by Brian Swisher.

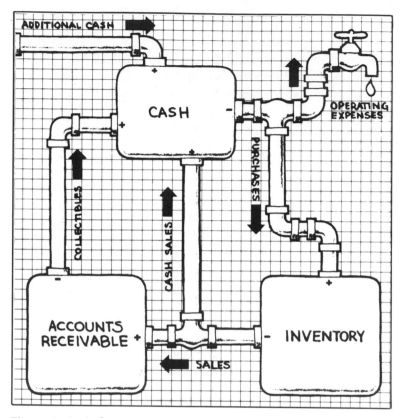

Figure 1. Cash-flow plumbing

to flow through the pipes and fill the reservoirs. It is all money energy, but it changes form as it moves through the business.

Assume that this business is a small retail store that rents its space and equipment. Merchandise is purchased for resale. Money energy from the cash reservoir flows into the inventory reservoir. When sales take place the money energy in inventory is converted into accounts receivable (for credit sales) or back into cash. When customers pay their accounts, the money energy is converted back into cash, completing the cycle. Cash will also flow out of the business to pay operating expenses, repay loans, and provide the owner with withdrawals or dividends.

This cycle is continuous as the business operates through

time and therefore is called the operating cycle. The reservoirs act as buffers between the operations taking place and work to support these operations. Therefore, the total money energy in the system is known as working capital.

Figure 2 shows the operating cycle and cash flow plumbing for a slightly more complex and typical situation. The same basic flow takes place, but trade credit (accounts payable) is used as a temporary source of money energy to help fill and support the inventory reservoir. Such use of trade credit reduces the total amount of owners' money energy tied up in supporting operations.

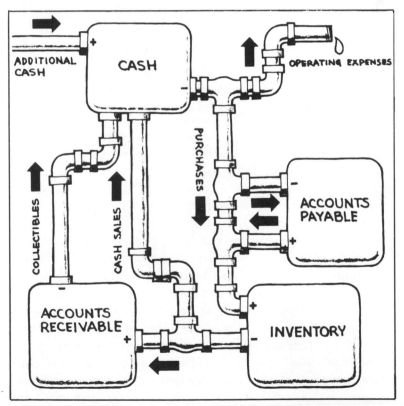

Figure 2. Cash-flow plumbing with trade credit (accounts payable)

Working capital is also often defined as current assets (cash, inventory, and accounts receivable) less current liabilities (accounts payable and other short-term payables). This figure, also called net working capital, measures the total amount of permanent capital invested in the support of the operating cycle. Do not be deceived by the words *current* and *short term*, however. These working capital reservoirs must maintain a certain minimum level of money energy at all times or the business cannot operate efficiently, if at all. Even though the form of the money energy is constantly changing or turning over, the total needed remains relatively constant. Working capital is every bit as much a permanent capital requirement for a business as are its so-called fixed assets (land, buildings, machinery, and equipment).

Narrowly defined, cash flow is the change in cash over a period of time, or the difference between cash flowing into the cash reservoir and that flowing out. But understanding and managing cash flow requires a knowledge of the operating cycle and the reservoirs and flows that comprise it.

The diagrams show that there is a lag between when cash flows out to purchase inventory and pay operating expenses and when that money energy completes its cycle and returns as cash. The length of the operating cycle is a critical determinant of the amount of money energy required for working capital.

Cash flow management often involves measures that influence the length of the operating cycle and the amount of time that money energy must spend in the various working capital reservoirs. Basically, any steps that can speed up the operating cycle will also speed up the cash flow and thus reduce the total amount of money energy required to support operations.

Different types of businesses have different operating cycles; so their cash flow plumbing will look different and the amount of working capital required to support a given level of operations will also differ. Generalizations about cash flow are somewhat difficult and possibly misleading. You must look at each business individually and study its operating cycle to determine how that company's cash flow plumbing should work and what its working capital should be.

For example, a restaurant can usually operate with a relatively small inventory. The perishable nature of food requires a quick turnover as much as it does management policy. Since all restaurant sales will be for cash or credit card, no accounts receivable are required. Thus, restaurants have a "fast" cash flow and need relatively less working capital than most businesses. The cash flow plumbing for a restaurant is depicted in Figure 3.

A retail clothing store will have a "slower" cash flow and

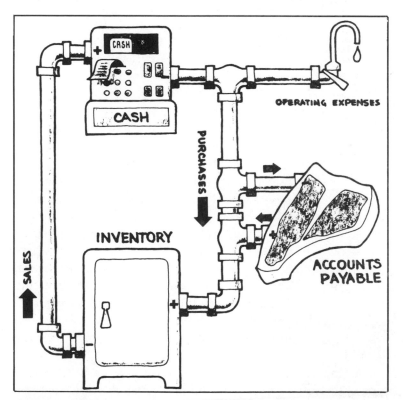

Figure 3. Cash flow in a restaurant

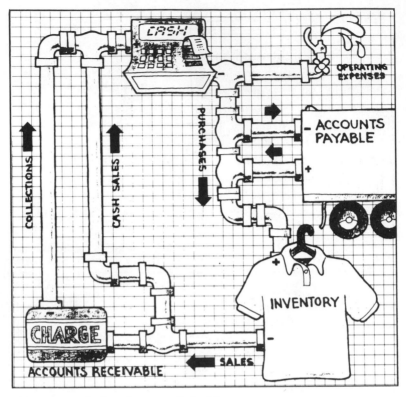

Figure 4. Cash flow in a retail clothing store

need more working capital. Inventories must be large so that customers can have a wide selection. Credit may be extended to certain customers to increase sales; money energy will be tied up in accounts receivable. The resulting cash flow pattern is presented in Figure 4.

A winery must carry large inventories because of the long production and aging process. Even if it can keep accounts receivable to a minimum through tight credit and prompt collection, it will have a long operating cycle and "slow" cash flow. The cash flow plumbing for a winery is characterized in Figure 5.

A magazine publisher has a much different cash flow situation. Much of the cash comes in *before* production (once the magazine has achieved its subscriber base) in the form of

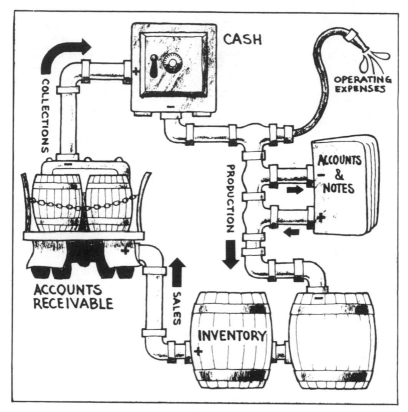

Figure 5. Cash flow in a small winery

advertising and subscription revenue. It could have sizable accounts receivable, but probably inventories are relatively small. Figure 6 suggests how this cash flow plumbing might look.

Each company has its own unique cash flow plumbing, partly determined by the nature of the business but also influenced by the financial policies and decisions of its owners or manager. You may find it valuable to draw a diagram of your own company's cash flow plumbing. Think of the steps in your business operating cycle and use the examples shown here as a guide. Add explanatory notes to the reservoirs and flows as has been done in the examples.

The process of thinking about and drawing your company's

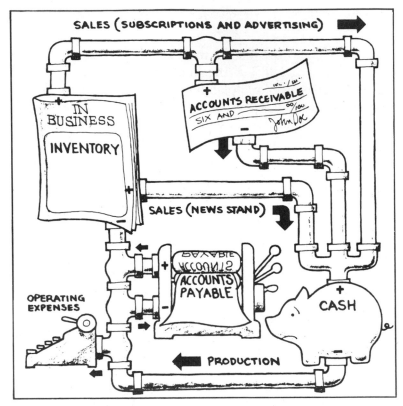

Figure 6. Cash flow for a magazine publisher

cash flow plumbing should integrate and increase your understanding of how money energy is (and isn't) working in your business. Even though what you draw is a static model, think of the dynamic process it represents: How will the reservoirs and flows change over time? The insight gained from this exercise can be substantial. You should discover exactly why an increase in your sales volume will create increased need for working capital. The value of inventory control and its impact on cash flow should become more apparent. The consequences of a change in your credit and collection policies should be easier to analyze. You may even spot ways to improve your cash flow and free up some of the money energy tied up in working capital.

A second important benefit to be gained by doing this exercise is that it establishes the kind of conceptual base that makes the analytical and planning tools of financial management easier to understand and relate to your own company. Working capital analysis, use of financial ratios, cash budgeting, and similar tools will make more sense and can be applied judiciously rather than mechanically.

8

The Growing Support Network

About ten independently owned laundries scattered over several Midwestern states have been organized into a miniature trade association. The owners meet several times a year, alternating locations, and analyze each other's businesses, criticizing performances and trading information.

In the crafts field, regional organizations bring together potters and candlemakers, weavers, and other artisans, offering seminars on pricing, marketing, and apprenticeships. "Most craftspeople who fail do so because they suffer from a lack of relevant information," a veteran silversmith declared during our discussion of small business developments. "What we need are more collective solutions to individual problems."

We recently helped to organize a Small Magazine Publishers Association, after our contacts with fellow publishers indicated a need to share ideas with others working with comparable numbers of readers, advertisers, and staff. Just about all of us attend the major industry meetings, but most discussions there are aimed at publishers with far larger circulations and many more promotional dollars to expend. In the words of one of our founding members, "We're tired of picking up the crumbs of ideas that fall down from the mass marketing layers."

New organizations—often quite informal—have been developing in recent years to meet the needs of small businesspersons. Some are regional, some are based upon similar businesses. All reflect the fact that the old organizations—the old Chambers of Commerce and Small Business Administration—don't meet current demands.

In Philadelphia, the Cooperative Association of Proprietors (CAP) was started in 1978. The merchants, restaurateurs, and other businesspeople who have joined CAP are for the most part young or new to business. Of the more than ninety members, nearly all have been in business less than ten years. Although all but twelve have annual sales of less than $500,-000, their combined sales exceed $25 million, the equivalent of a major enterprise, making CAP more than the sum of its parts. Notes CAP President Steve Poses, "Any $25 million business would have built into it a marketing department, an insurance department, a legal department, and so forth that no individual proprietor could afford. But by getting together, because of the scale we can achieve, we suddenly have access to new alternatives that small businesses can't afford alone."

Five general membership meetings each year, a monthly newsletter, and periodic seminars offer CAP members practical advice on such topics as financing, parking, zoning, security, advertising, personnel interviewing, first aid, lease negotiations, window display, and promotions. They also help to foster a vital sense of cohesion among the businesses involved by providing an organizational identity as well as passing along information about the members' varied business activities.

One example of the promotional effort put together by CAP is the campaign, "There's No Shopping Center Like Shopping Center City." A map was produced, showing the location of members' establishments. Displayed by members and distributed by center city hotels, the map has turned out to be a very effective business-building tool. Also important to CAP members are such things as cooperative buying of supplies at discount, collective purchase of insurance, and the periodic seminars.

FINANCING NETWORKS

Besides information sharing and market coordination, some of the new support efforts even get into the area of informal risk capital, helping in the search for "friendly money." Under the direction of Professor William Wetzel, the University of New Hampshire's Center for Industrial and Institutional Development launched a research effort in 1980 "to determine the cost and availability of informal risk capital for firms without access to traditional venture capital sources or the public equity markets." The research aims to improve the availability of risk capital for inventors, entrepreneurs, and dynamic small firms and to increase the opportunities available to risk capital investors. Wetzel believes that some of the best prospects in the second category may themselves have been fledgling entrepreneurs some years back but are now successful and understanding of young firms.

For the researchers at the University of New Hampshire, gathering data on informal investors will help to strengthen the small business base in New England. "As far as I know, no one else has tried to identify informal risk capital in an organized way, yet we see this search for friendly money as a key to our economic strategy for revitalizing New England small businesses," explains Wetzel. When investors were asked in the survey if they would accept a lower rate of return on their investment if the opportunity had a socioeconomic impact, such as creating jobs or developing a new technology with social benefit, the response was unusually high in favor of these nonfinancial rewards.

In addition, Wetzel and associates see their efforts as having a catalytic effect, eventually mobilizing the private sector to make funds more available to growing enterprises. "There's a need for a catalyst in this area right now, because the potential benefits tend to be public—to help the local community. If we can show that monies can be pooled for this kind of investment and returns are satisfactory, then we can expect private investment firms to develop in the future."

The UNH research effort is being funded by the U.S. Small Business Administration's Office of Economic Development. One mechanism the UNH staff envisions creating is a referral service for investors and entrepreneurs. "We can see setting up some sort of a referral/screening service through which investors and entrepreneurs can be paired," explains Craig Seymour, assistant director of the survey project. "For example, there are now innovation centers at several universities in the United States. These centers are set up to help inventors test the viability and marketability of their inventions. This could be one phase of the referral service—screening inventor-entrepreneurs. The next phase is keeping a file of investors and their areas of interest. That way, if someone comes up with a new silicon chip for a computer and it's found to be marketable, we would then get that person together with an investor interested in computer technology. Preliminary survey results showed a strong interest in this referral service."

The survey revealed a strong network that exists among these informal investors. They are aligned by geographic area or area of investment but also cross over from one area to another.

EDUCATIONAL OPPORTUNITIES

Glance through the catalogs of today's business schools and you'll see that these colleges and universities are the training grounds for chief executives of *Fortune* 500 companies.

Course titles read like subjects for corporate boardroom discussions.

More than 400 U.S. universities now offer graduate programs in business, an increase of over 125 in ten years. Enrollments have more than doubled in the last decade, from 76,000 to 175,000. MBAs are awarded at an annual rate of 50,000. Just about every major business school, however, puts almost all its major emphasis on big business. Defending that position, Carol Walnum, placement director for Northwestern University's Business School, says: "Our orientation reflects the overwhelming preference for large corporations that our graduates show in their first jobs. We suspect that the budding entrepreneurs among our students seek out their opportunities later in their business lives."

But, if you take a closer look at the business school catalogs, you'll find evidence of a new trend: courses that are well suited to the training of independent SBOs—small business owners—instead of only CEOs—chief executive officers.

When Karl Vesper of the University of Washington first began tracking courses in entrepreneurship offered by U.S. schools back in 1967, he came up with a list of 10. In 1980, when he published a revised edition of his report, *Entrepreneurship Education,* Vesper's list had climbed to more than 140.

Historically, business schools have perceived themselves as the private hunting grounds of large corporations that make regular campus treks to scout for fresh supplies of bright young managers. Course offerings have naturally been geared toward the needs of these corporations, teaching the complexities of corporate policies and politics. Why then this new crop of studies in small business ownership and venture start-ups?

According to Vesper, a catalyst himself for more entrepreneurial education, student demand—not school policy—is responsible. Many faculty continue to view corporate management as the sole purpose of business programs and to consider small business as nothing more than "mom-and-pop-ism." Courses in small business management seem, to these academics, to conflict with the school's intentions.

As for entrepreneurial studies, many academics, both proponents and detractors of the subject, question whether any course or curriculum can actually teach entrepreneurship. "Aren't business-formers born with certain predisposing personality traits?" they ask. "What body of knowledge is available to teach prospective entrepreneurs?"

In actuality, few courses are intended to "make" entrepreneurs. Research shows that indeed certain personalities are better suited than others for entrepreneurial careers, and the strong belief prevails that traditionally independent business persons have been able to succeed quite well without any formal schooling. Thus, most programs and courses serve to introduce students to problems of new ventures and, in some cases, to help students decide if they are capable of handling them.

At Babson College, located just outside of Boston, students must demonstrate entrepreneurial potential before they are admitted to courses. According to Dr. John Hornaday, chairman of the college's Division of Management which offers a major in entrepreneurial studies, "You can't teach entrepreneurship in total because so much depends on a student's inherited characteristics. But to be a successful entrepreneur, you must have knowledge. You don't necessarily have to be technically trained, but you have to know the decision-making procedures. Those can be taught. We can increase the probability of success." According to Vesper, National Science Foundation grants to MIT, Carnegie-Mellon University, University of Oregon, and University of Utah for the creation of innovation centers encouraged those schools to introduce courses in entrepreneurship.

Today, nearly 150 schools offer one or more courses in starting and operating small businesses. Each year, some 3,000 to 4,000 students take these courses at schools ranging from two-year junior and technical colleges to four-year universities. Even Harvard offers a new ventures program, with half an MBA class of 750 students enrolled in the basic course and some 30 to 40 of those going on to write their field study reports on possible new business ventures.

At most schools, these courses take a definite back seat to more traditional ones. Students are usually encouraged to combine courses with concentration in management, real estate, marketing, accounting, finance, or other fields in order to enable them to enter a variety of jobs.

It is not always easy to fit such courses into the larger scheme of the curriculum and to define their areas of concern. Some universities offer the courses through the business policy or management department, whereas others squeeze them into financing and marketing. At a considerable number of institutions, engineering departments (particularly creative design and mechanical engineering) handle entrepreneurial studies.

Full undergraduate and graduate degree programs in entrepreneurship are beginning to spring up at various schools. Babson College has recently begun offering an undergraduate major for students "who seek to become entrepreneurs or who wish to work with entrepreneurs in some special capacity such as consultant, financial analyst, or venture capitalist." Baylor University in Waco, Texas, offers a similar program designed to teach students to identify potentially attractive new ventures, define capital and other sources, and start, sell, or merge a business interest. Northeastern Oregon State, Harvard, Wharton, Southern Methodist, University of Southern California, and others offer similar undergraduate and/or graduate programs in entrepreneurship.

Most programs begin with a basic, general entrepreneurship course. Students are given a historical view of entrepreneurship and are taught how to obtain venture capital, acquire another firm, make a business plan, protect ideas, hire and fire, advertise, figure taxes, and make economic projections.

Virtually all such courses require a venture design project, a kind of field assignment in which the student searches out his or her own business idea. For even more hands-on experience, some offer internships whereby students work directly in small businesses for a period of two weeks to one year, depending on the program.

A program established by the Small Business Administration, called the Small Business Institute (SBI), has a similar role in providing practical experience for seniors and graduate-level students. This program is geared specifically toward students of business who are interested in becoming either entrepreneurs or counselors to them. Through an SBI, students furnish free, on-site management counseling to owners on a semester basis. The students are guided by a faculty member and an SBA management assistance officer, receiving course credit for the semester-long program. The businesses to which the students are assigned include both those receiving loans from the SBA and nonclients. They represent all aspects of the business community.

Started as a pilot program at 36 schools in the fall of 1972, the SBI now has 455 participating institutions of higher learning located in all of the fifty states, the District of Columbia, Puerto Rico, and Guam. Annually some 2,000 SBI professors and 20,000 students work with 8,000 firms in all phases of management, such as marketing research, cost analysis, product and service promotion, accounting, building or shop design, and efficiency studies. At the end of the semester, final reports including an analysis of the business with recommendations for implementation are prepared and given to the owner.

Formal internship is just a small part of the first-hand experience that craft students gain at North Country Community College in upstate New York. Through internships as well as classroom training, students earning an Associate in Applied Science degree in crafts management receive a unique blend of business and art training. The school is located in the restored Ballard Mill Center for the Arts, where craftspersons have their shops. Students are constantly watching young businesses take off. They see advertising, production, fiscal management, and personnel management all taking place around them. Says Douglas Kelly, former director of the Malone Extension of North Country Community College and founder of the program, "Because of the facilities, which really made the program visible (in terms of limited expense), there is a lot of room for innovation in course offerings and valuable 'in-house' experience through working with craftspeople at the Ballard Mill Center for the Arts."

Crafts courses at the school include pottery, blacksmithing, jewelry making, weaving, and quilting. Business courses include accounting, marketing principles, business law, business management, and business communications.

For businesspersons and potential entrepreneurs not seeking a formal degree, many of these schools offer special seminars, workshops, and programs that provide the same practical help and education. The Division of Management at Babson and the Center for Private Enterprise and Entrepreneurship at Baylor both offer not-for-credit courses that increase the skills needed for business success. The University of California at Santa Cruz runs a Center for Innovation and Entrepreneurial Development, which offers courses on starting business ventures and workshops and seminars with distinguished outside speakers. Similarly, the innovation centers at MIT, Carnegie-Mellon, Oregon, and Utah all provide courses and seminars for the aspiring entrepreneur.

Small Business Development Centers, government-sponsored university outreach similar to the SBI programs, offer business assistance similar to that offered to farmers through the agricultural extension program. Administered through the Small Business Administration, they offer professional help at no charge to small-business owners and entrepreneurs. In a sense, they operate like management consulting firms able to draw on the services of the full university system.

In addition to general counseling and management assistance, each center gears itself toward the problems faced by the small business sector in their state and/or region. For example, the SBDC in Maine focuses on improving the state's timber industry, while the Rutgers University center concentrates on the problems of inner city decay.

Whether or not entrepreneurship can actually be "taught" remains debatable, and, indeed, many hard-line academics continue to scoff at today's entrepreneurial education programs. But for the person in business seeking help and advice, or for the potential entrepreneur requiring technical information on business formation and management, these programs, whether in school or out, seem to offer the range of practical, technical information needed.

REGIONAL ASSOCIATIONS

Besides informal networks and grass-roots organizations to assist start-up and developing businesses, there's an increasing number of more formal associations. One, for example, has been called a "business support system for women only"—the American Woman's Economic Development Corporation (AWED) in New York City. AWED provides free training, assistance, and counseling to women business owners and women planning businesses in the New York City area. A strong feature is the sharing of experiences by women who gained valuable knowledge when they started out themselves and who offer to counsel others.

In the Boston area, the Small Business Association of New England holds a series of useful seminars on many subjects for members. In California, the Continental Association of Resolute Employers—CARE—brings members an informative publication, insurance programs, legislative updates, and the like.

As described earlier in this chapter, Philadelphia shopkeepers formed the Cooperative Association of Proprietors for common problem solving; the New Hampshire Craftsmen Guild is typical of many regional marketing organizations for craftspersons. One in Maine, HOME (Homeworkers Organized for More Employment), opened up three retail outlets in urban locations as a way to increase sales.

Small-business persons are characterized by a strong streak of independence, but often some organizations, especially the regional, specially focused ones, are proving to be of value.

Part of the support network—maybe the most important part—comes from the people who are in business now. For the most part, you'll find people willing to share information such as the names of a particularly helpful lawyer or accountant. The important point is to ask. It's often that simple. The more secretive you are, the more trouble you'll have.

There are all kinds of accounting services, training sessions, counseling individuals, and companies. Be selective, and be patient in deciding which ones are right for you.

Afterword

Some time ago, we attended a lecture at a nearby university on entrepreneurship along with some friends who have their own business. The speaker animatedly recounted the glorious history of venture start-ups and the characteristics of today's commercial innovators. A few days later, I received a phone call around 7 PM from one of the persons who was at the lecture: "Quick, Jerry, tell me again how great it is to have your own business. I still have at least another two hours to go tonight!"

And so it goes with small businesses—and it goes better as long as you keep your sense of humor out front. I'm convinced a sense of humor and balance are critical to success.

It's been three years since we joined the new American business movement. Thinking back to when we first arranged to rent our office and postal box, I don't recall our feeling that what we were doing was part of a movement; the move just seemed logical and worthwhile. And it still does. I had just finished more than twenty-five years with a company, enjoyed being part of its development from an unprofitable beginning to a profitable 60-million-dollar-a-year enterprise. But it was becoming increasingly clear to me that my satisfaction from being with a successful company was related more to innovation than profit maximization. It was time to split, with great memories, rather than to hang on with great salaries.

So, rather abruptly, the move was made and there I was, along with five others, including several family members. Since the first day we set up the JG Press, there's been little time for dreaming.

After a few years, we have some major accomplishments to show for our efforts. First, as most of our fellow entrepreneurs will attest, our major feat in the eyes of many is that we're still around. We now are publishing two bimonthly magazines with steadily growing readership and have published four books and sponsored a series of seminars on topics related to our editorial coverage. We have not yet reached a million-dollar annual sales figure—nor do we have 100,000 subscribers to either *In Business* or *BioCycle*—but we have consistently increased in all categories that a publisher uses to measure progress: circulation, renewals, advertising income, and the like. But there still are only a few of us doing the work—the editing, subscription promotion and fulfillment, sales, and so on. A small staff that does everything from the menial to the creative is initially the best defense—and offense—in a young business. No worry about the rate, quality, or quantity of American productivity in the few-person shop.

Keeping up with our business means keeping busy, not getting too far behind schedule, and doing our own kind of hustling in a way that feels comfortable. We hustle to get new readers, to obtain good editorial material, to reach potential advertisers. It's the same kind of hustle that just about every new entrepreneur goes through today. And the sum of all the activity makes the effort worthwhile.

There may or may not be a pot of gold at the end of our personal rainbow—I'm not sure if I'll ever know for certain.

But that uncertainty doesn't take away from my desire to make what we're doing work. Nor does the lack of a guarantee affect the thousands and thousands out there living out their own scenarios. As far as I can tell, we won't have it any other way, now that we've had our share of the independent, good life of making it on our own.

Appendix:
New Small Business
Directory

Businessmen and businesswomen, I find, love to talk about business. Business is a large part of their lives, and they love to share their experiences and their ideas. You can't get better advice at any price; no accountant or lawyer or college professor knows half of what the person who's doing it every day knows. Strike up acquaintances, get to be friends with business people, find out about their local merchants organizations and attend their luncheons.

—Bernard Kamoroff
author of *Small Time Operator:*
How to Start Your Own Small Business, Keep Your
Books, Pay Your Taxes, and Stay Out of Trouble
(Bell Springs Pub., 1980)

Associations, Lobby Groups, Trade Associations

Accountants for the Public Interest
Fort Mason Center
Building 310, 3rd Floor
San Francisco, CA 94123
Clearinghouse on activities and organizations of accountants concerned with wide variety of public interest issues.

American Association of Small Research Companies
8794 West Chester Pike
Upper Darby, PA 19082
Matches up small R&D companies with potential large contractors by organizing conferences.

American Wind Energy Association
1609 Connecticut Ave., N.W.
Washington, DC 20009
Trade association for wind energy businesses; lobby group.

Briarpatch Network
330 Ellis St.
San Francisco, CA 94102
Based on barter between businesses. Networking; see *Briarpatch Book* (New Glide, $8.00).

Center for Family Businesses
University Services Institute
P.O. Box 24268
Cleveland, OH 44124
Membership organization for family-owned businesses. Seminars, newsletter.

Continental Association of Resolute Employers
555 Northgate Drive
San Rafael, CA 94903
Membership association for small and medium-sized businesses. Insurance program, seminars, publications.

Human Economy Center
P.O. Box 551
Amherst, MA 01004
Membership organization with local chapters. Newsletter; organizes seminars around appropriate technologies and other small businesses.

National Association of Small Business Investment Companies
618 Washington Building
Washington, DC 20005
Trade association for SBA-licensed venture capital investment companies. Newsletter on venture capital.

National Association of Women Business Owners
2000 P St., N.W.
Washington, DC 20036
Has many local chapters to assist women entrepreneurs. Newsletter, workshops, lobbies.

National Association of Women in Commerce
1333 Howe Ave., Suite 210
Sacramento, CA 95825
Membership association for women in career planning or business start-ups. Workshops.

National Federation of Independent Business
150 W. 20th Ave.
San Mateo, CA 94403
Small business association with over 600,000 members; strong Washington lobby with Washington office.

National Small Business Association
1604 K St., N.W.
Washington, DC 20006
Membership association, lobbying group. Procurement search service, newsletters.

National Venture Capital Association
2030 M St., N.W., Suite 403
Washington, DC 20036
Trade association for venture capital professionals.

Rural American Women, Inc.
1522 K St., N.W., Suite 700
Washington, DC 20005
Membership association for rural women. Includes assistance to women entrepreneurs, co-ops.

Small Business Foundation of America
69 Hickory Drive
Waltham, MA 02154
Gives and receives research grants, conducts seminars, does regional and federal advocacy.

Small Business Service Bureau
544 Main St., Box 1441
Worcester, MA 01601
Membership association effective in retail trades and five-or-less employee businesses. Offers insurance packages and monthly magazine.

Solar Energy Institute of North America
1110 6th St., N.W.
Washington, DC 20001
Membership association/lobby group. Developing markets for U.S. solar companies abroad.

Solar Lobby
1001 Connecticut Ave., N.W., Suite 510
Washington, DC 20036

Lobbies for solar, including solar energy businesses. Newsletter and $15 membership.

Women Working at Home
145 N. 9th Ave.
Highland Park, NJ 08904

Researches women working at home. Published *Home-Based Business Guide and Directory* ($14.20), $25 membership.

Business Counseling and Assistance

Accion International
10-C Mt. Auburn St.
Cambridge, MA 02138
Microbusiness development. Workshops, small expansion loans for projects in Maine.

American Women's Economic Development Corporation
1270 Avenue of Americas
New York, NY 10020
Courses and counseling for women entrepreneurs.

Center for Innovation
P.O. Box 3809
Butte, MT 59701
Evaluates/tests inventions, assists with marketing if feasible. Federally funded, already introduced products with worth over $75 million.

National Solar Heating and Cooling Center
P.O. Box 1607, Dept. LB
Rockville, MD 20850
(800) 523-2929
Data bank for solar businesses. Matches up consumer with producer/seller, supplies technical information.

New Ways to Work
457 Kingley Ave.
Palo Alto, CA 94301
Provides workshops and directory on doing business from home.

Resources for Women
104 Walnut Ave., Suite 212
Santa Cruz, CA 95060
Published *Establishing Your Business: A Handbook For Women and Women's Yellow Pages*. Counseling and assistance services available.

Small Business Development Center
Small Business Administration
1441 L St., N.W.
Washington, DC 20416
Sixteen university-based technical assistance centers. Workshops, counseling.

Small Farm Energy Project
Center for Rural Affairs
P.O. Box 736
Hartington, NE 68739

Research on small farm technologies and energy. Supports family farm issues.

University Business Development Centers
Small Business Administration
1441 L St., N.W.
Washington, DC 20416
University-based technical assistance. Nine centers.

Business Development Groups

A.T. International
1709 N St., N.W.
Washington, DC 20036
Assists businesses in developing nations. Develops appropriate technologies.

Corporation for Enterprise Development
2420 K St., N.W.
Washington, DC 20037
Development finance research group, targeted at small business creation.

Institute for Local Self-Reliance
1717 18th St., N.W.
Washington, DC 20009
Neighborhood-based assistance. Researches business opportunities, e.g., waste recycling, conservation, solar energy.

Institute for New Enterprise Development
17 Dunster St.
Cambridge, MA 02138
Venture development services to community groups that are creating or expanding businesses.

Kentucky Highlands Investment Corporation
P.O. Box 628
London, KY 40741
Venture capitalist-oriented economic development firm that makes investments in small businesses in southeastern Kentucky.

Entrepreneurial Education

Association for Chairs of Private Enterprise
Craig Aranoff, President
School of Business
Georgia State University
Atlanta, GA 30303
Write for list of schools with academic chairs in fields of entrepreneurship and free enterprise.

Babson College
Entrepreneurial Studies Program
Babson Park, Wellesley, MA 02157
Entrepreneurial studies; graduate and undergraduate degree programs.

Center for Industrial and Institutional Development
University of New Hampshire
Durham, NH 03824
Identifies availability of informal risk capital in New England.

Center for Venture Management
207 E. Buffalo St.
Milwaukee, WI 53202

Write for detailed list of schools and course descriptions on new ventures and entrepreneurship.

Entrepreneurship Education in 1980
By Karl H. Vesper
University of Washington
Graduate School of Business Administration
Seattle, WA 98195
Catalog of all courses in entrepreneurship, about 100 schools. $10.

Hankamer School of Business
Baylor University
Waco, TX 76703
Offers degree program in entrepreneurial studies.

International Council for Small Business Management
University of Wisconsin, Extension
929 N. 6th Street
Milwaukee, WI 53203
Membership association for academicians in fields of small business management.

Federal Government Resources

Congressional Clearinghouse for the Future
3564 House Annex No. 2
Washington, DC 20515
Progressive congressional group with informative newsletter on wide range of economic and governmental issues.

Directory of State Small Business Programs, 1980 Edition
Small Business Administration
Washington, DC 20416
State-by-state breakdown of loan, procurement, technical assistance programs, and more.

Federal Trade Commission
Washington, DC 20580
Write for listing of regulations affecting your industry, e.g., textiles, packaging.

House Small Business Committee
2361 Rayburn House Office Building
Washington, DC 20515
Official legislators on small business issues.

Internal Revenue Service
Washington, DC 20224
Free tax handbooks plus free seminars. Write for local listings.

International Trade Administration
Business Counseling Section
Office of Export Development
Room 4009
Department of Commerce
Washington, DC 20230
Export assistance.

Minority Business Development Agency
Public Affairs Office
Department of Commerce
14th and Constitution, N.W.
Washington, DC 20230
Many regional and local offices. Technical assistance and financing for minority-owned businesses. Publishes free bimonthly, *Access,* with new laws, resources, and profiles.

National Center for Appropriate Technology
P.O. Box 3838
Butte, MT 58701
Research grants for many appropriate technology businesses: recycling, energy, health, farming. Offers good technical reports.

National Science Foundation
Small Business Innovation Office
1800 G St., N.W.
Washington, DC 20550
Research grants, patent assistance, workshops, reports.

National Technical Information Service
Department of Commerce
5285 Port Royal Road
Springfield, VA 22161
R&D arm of federal government. Write for report catalog.

Patent and Trademark Office
Department of Commerce
Washington, DC 20231
Free booklets on patents and inventions.

Register of Copyrights
Library of Congress
Washington, DC 20540
Free information on copyrights.

Security and Exchange Commission
Office of Small Business Policy
500 N. Capitol St.
Washington, DC 20549
Rules and regulations for public or private stock offerings. Write for free pamphlet, "Q&A: Small Business and SEC".

Senate Small Business Committee
424 Russell Office Building
Washington, DC 20510
Legislative committee for overall small business issues.

Small Business Administration
1441 L St., N.W.
Washington, DC 20416
Main government agency for small business. Offices include Advocacy, Procurement, Lending, Technical/Management Assistance, Publications.

Publications

Business Planning Guide
Upstart Publishing Company
366 Islington St.
Portsmouth, NH 03801
Popular business plan book.

Craft Resources
Economics, Statistics and Cooperative Services
GHI Building, Room 550
Department of Agriculture
Washington, DC 20250
Free publication listing federal resources for crafts development and more.

Directory of Lawyer Referral Services
Legal Services Group
Standing Committee on Lawyer Referral Services
American Bar Association
1155 E. 60th Street
Chicago, IL 60637
List of state and local bar organizations that provide referral services and guide to their use. $5.

Encyclopedia of Business Information Sources
Gale Research Company
Book Tower
Detroit, MI 48226
Over 1,280 specific subject areas. Good library reference. $94.

Franchising and the Law
Director of Membership Services
1025 Connecticut Ave., N.W., Suite 1005
Washington, DC 20036
Pamphlet on franchising your business. $10.

In Business
JG Press, Inc.
Emmaus, PA 18049
Magazine specializes in new business management, profiles creative entrepreneurs. $14/year subscription.

Management Aids
Small Business Administration
P.O. Box 15434
Fort Worth, TX 76119
(800) 433-7212
Hundreds of management-aid pamphlets from the SBA.

New Venture Strategies
By Karl Vesper
Prentice-Hall
Englewood Cliffs, NJ 07632
Variety of venture start-up options with good case studies. $10.95 (paper), $16.95 (cloth).

Small Business: Look Before You Leap
By Louis Mucciolo
Arco Publishing, Inc.
219 Park Ave. South
New York, NY 10003
Catalog of information sources for starting and managing. $8.95.

Small Business Reporter
Bank of America
Dept. No. 3120
P.O. Box 37000
San Francisco, CA 94137
Short how-to guides on a variety of businesses, from crafts to publishing. $2.

Small Time Operator
By Bernard Kamoroff
Bell Springs Publishing
P.O. Box 640
Laytonville, CA 95454
Guide for start-ups; annual up-
dates. $8.80.

Seminars

Center for Entrepreneurial
Management
311 Main St.
Worcester, MA 01608
Newsletter, seminars, work-
shops.

Country Business Services
22 Main St.
Brattleboro, VT 05301
Seminars for starting/buying
an operating business.

The East-West Center
1777 East-West Road
Honolulu, HI 96848
Seminars in identifying and developing entrepreneurial
capabilities.

The Entrepreneurship Institute
90 E. Wilson Bridge Road,
Suite 247
Worthington, OH 43085
Courses for entrepreneurs.

New School for Democratic
Management
589 Howard St.
San Francisco, CA 94108
Offers courses in co-op man-
agement and more.

The School for Entrepreneurs
Tarrytown House
East Sunnyside Lane
Tarrytown, NY 10591
Specializing in New Age busi-
ness attitudes; directed by
Robert Schwartz.

Uncollege Management Training Center
P.O. Box 736
Point Pleasant, NJ 08742
Counseling on marketing, ad-
advertising, packaging, time
management, etc.

State Financing Sources

Alaska Renewable Resource
  Corporation
526 Main St.
Juneau, AK 99802
Financing available for start-
ups and expansion. Technical assistance. Develops local
resources.

Cal-Rural
1044 Fulton Mall, No. 506
Fresno, CA 93721
Financing for small businesses,
farms, co-ops.

Coastal Enterprises, Inc.
14 Front St.
Bath, ME 04530
Technical assistance, financing
for businesses that develop
local resources, e.g., fisher-
ies, sheep growing. Serves
several Maine counties.

Massachusetts Community Development Finance Corporation
131 State St.
Boston MA 02109
Finances businesses developing
community resources.

Urban Initiatives

Cooperative Association of
  Proprietors
1175 17th St., Room 315
Philadelphia, PA 19103
Merchants' association to improve sales. Provides workshops, supports revival of
downtown.

Local Initiatives Support
  Corporation
666 3rd Ave.
New York, NY 10017

Provides loans to community
organizations involved in
revitalization.

Pike Place Market Preserva-
tion and Development Au-
thority
85 Pike St., Room 500
Seattle, WA 98101
Urban economic revitalization,
using local small businesses.
Created a downtown farm-
ers and craft market.

South Shore National Bank
Neighborhood Development
  Center
71st and Jeffrey Blvd.
Chicago, IL 60649
Credit department for development lending, greenlining neighborhoods.

Whiteaker Community Council
21 N. Grand
Eugene, OR 97402
Neighborhood economic revitalization with appropriate technologies.

Index

Date Due

MAR 1 6 1984 APR 1 8 2006			
FEB 1 7 1989			
OCT 2 0 1989			
NOV 1 5 1991			
JAN 2 6 1993			
NOV 2 3 1993			
FEB 0 6 1996			
MAR 2 7 1996 OCT 2 4 1997			
NOV 0 5 1999			

176 / *Index*

Toffler, Alvin, 4
tradition, 111

Vesper, Karl, 20, 131

waste recycling businesses
  Ad+Soil, 90
  BioGro Systems, 91
  Clivus Multrum, 86
  Crate Prospects, 92
  Domestic Environmental
    Alternatives, 87
  New Mullbank, 87
  Solar Aqua Systems, 89
Webster, Frederick E., 8
Wells, Malcolm, 104
Wetzel, William, 128,
  146

Whiteside, Thomas, 9
wind machines, 101
women business owners
  Collette, Marian, 123
  Hazel, Linda, 71
  Johnson, Natalie, 40
  Jones, Brook, 58
  Levitt, Carol, 64
  Radcliff, Barbara, 53
  Rick, Nan, 51
  Riecken, Susan, 57
  Rumschlag, Catherine,
    122
  Swaim, Karen, 38
  Wallas, Eugenie, 33
  Wilson, Jane, 115
wood and coal stoves, 95
wooden boatbuilding, 107